# MARIPOSA CHILD PROGRAM
*Transforming the way communities raise children...*

## PROMOTING SOCIAL-EMOTIONAL COMPETENCE: MANAGING BEHAVIOR AND IMPROVING PERFORMANCE
### Companion Guide

www.MariposaEducation.org

---

1500 Union Ave., Baltimore, MD 21211 • telephone: 410.261.3740 • fax: 443.320.9280 • www.mariposaeducation.org

# MARIPOSA CHILD SUCCESS PROGRAMS

*Transforming the way communities raise children...*

1500 Union Ave., Baltimore, MD 21211 • telephone: 410.261.3740 • fax: 443.320.9280 • www.mariposaeducation.org

# Table of Contents

Introduction..................................................................................................01

Section 1: Orientation.................................................................................09

      Case Study/Action Plan..................................................................16

Section 2: Social-Emotional Competence..................................................19

      Handouts & Exercises.....................................................................27

          Four Interaction Styles............................................................28

          Reflection Questions...............................................................30

Section 3: Empathy......................................................................................31

      Handouts & Exercises.....................................................................38

          Empathy Handout...................................................................39

          15 Challenging Characters......................................................40

          Case Study/Action Plan..........................................................44

          Reflection Journal Questions..................................................46

Section 4: Personal Message.......................................................................47

      Handouts & Exercises.....................................................................53

          Personal Message Responses..................................................56

          15 Challenging Characters......................................................58

          Case Study/Action Plan..........................................................63

          Reflection Journal Questions..................................................64

Section 5: Cooperative Problem Solving....................................................65

      Handouts & Exercises.....................................................................72

          Cooperative Problem Solving Idea Sheet...............................73

          15 Challenging Characters......................................................74

      Building a Community of Support:

           Planning for Your Meeting............................................................83

           Case Study/Action Plan..............................................................85

           Reflection Journal Questions......................................................87

## Section 6: Descriptive Reinforcement ...............................................................89

      Handouts & Exercises...........................................................................96

           Praise vs. Encouragement..........................................................97

           15 Challenging Characters.........................................................98

           Case Study/Action Plan............................................................101

           Developing an Action Plan for Your Classroom........................103

           Reflection Journal Questions....................................................106

## Section 7: Inductive Discipline.......................................................................107

      Handouts & Exercises.........................................................................114

           15 Challenging Characters.......................................................115

           Restating the Rules...................................................................119

           Case Study/Action Plan............................................................120

           Reflection Journal Questions....................................................121

## Section 8: Fostering Systemic Change............................................................123

## Appendix........................................................................................................127

      Sequence of Skills...............................................................................128

      Recommended Reading......................................................................131

      Sample Answers..................................................................................135

## References.....................................................................................................153

# MARIPOSA CHILD SUCCESS PROGRAMS
*Transforming the way communities raise children...*

# Introduction

# Mariposa Child Success Programs

**About Mariposa**

*Our mission is to foster social-emotional competence (SEC) in children by training adults in key skills.* These skills cultivate a child's ability to develop *and* sustain a healthy relationship with the teacher, the family, and the community as a whole. Further, these skills enhance relationships between and among caregivers (i.e. parents, teachers, guardians), as positive teacher-teacher and parent-teacher relationships support the deepening of the adult-child relationship.

**The Mariposa Model: An Ecological Approach**

We know that adults are the single most effective means of enhancing a child's resilience and fostering their success in school and life. Since kids spend the majority of their time between school and home, training parents *and* educators brings consistency and teamwork to a child's development. We strive to bridge the gap between home life and school by fostering authentic, collaborative communication between school and home.

Our ecological approach trains the adults who are key influences in a child's life. The adults then become models, or *social-emotional coaches*, through practicing and perfecting the key skills. With practice, a reciprocal process begins wherein the children begin to absorb the skills taught by adults and in so doing build up social-emotional competencies themselves. In this way, a child's circle of positive influence begins to expand to his/her peer group, as the whole community is empowered to wrap itself around the child in ways that support and develop social-emotional competence.

**The Mariposa Method: 5 Essential Skills**

While conventional wisdom asserts 'kids do well if they want to,' Mariposa believes 'kids do well if they *can*.' That is, the challenging behaviors adults grapple with on a daily basis are often the result of underdeveloped social-emotional skills rather than a willful personality, ego, or ineffective parenting. We all have questions, concerns, and queries about how to effectively teach kids to consider others, work cooperatively, and hold themselves accountable to and responsible for choices made, all of which fall under the category of social-emotional competence.

The nonprofit organization CASEL (Collaborative for Academic, Social, and Emotional Learning), which works to advance the science and evidence-based practice of social and emotional learning, has identified five groups of skills that underlie SEC. The Mariposa Method incorporates these five groups of skills into its program. To cultivate social-emotional competence in children, we emphasize the use of these skills as tools of prevention—as a way to lessen the frequency and severity of crises and conflicts involving children. The first three skills (**Empathy**, **Personal Message**, and **Cooperative Problem Solving**) are sequential and lay the foundation for what we call a *helping relationship*. A helping relationship is an equitable way of forming trust and bonds with children to make SEC mentorship possible. The fourth skill, **Descriptive Reinforcement**, often comes as a result of Cooperative Problem Solving, while the fifth and final skill, **Inductive Discipline**, offers a fresh approach to behavior modification, one that underscores the link between negative behaviors and consequences. The skills are as follows:

- **Empathy (building trust and understanding)** – Adult mirrors child's concerns and/or feelings, building trust providing a basis for a helping relationship.
- **Personal Message (communicating feelings and expectations)** – Adult relays personal impact of a child's behavior on himself/herself and therefore promotes the child's social awareness.
- **Cooperative Problem Solving (working together toward mutually satisfying solutions)** – Adult and child work together to create mutually satisfying goals in response to a problem, thus modeling the how-to of responsible decision making, which considers all the people involved in a conflict.
- **Descriptive Reinforcement (fostering internal motivation)** - Adults describe a child's positive or negative behavior in observational terms without labels or judgment.
- **Inductive Discipline (promoting self-control)** - Adult acknowledges natural consequences and enforces logical consequences when necessary, thereby supporting a child's ability to make connections between personal behavior and consequences.

The more these skills are practiced with consistency across multiple sources of influence (e.g., by multiple teachers as well as the parents or caregivers of the child), the greater the positive impact on the child's well-being.

**Why Social-Emotional Competence?**
The answer is simple: children who demonstrate SEC are better able to handle themselves, develop healthy relationships, work ethically and effectively, and excel academically.

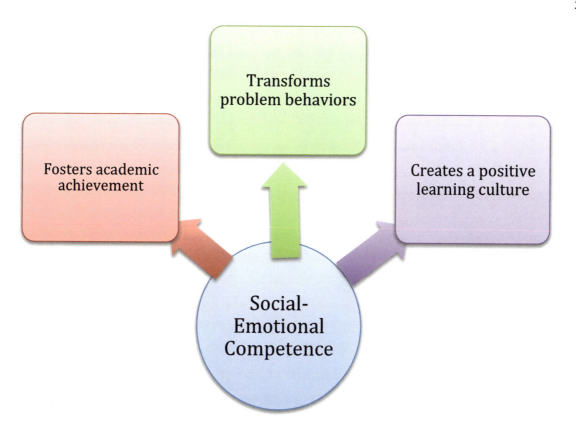

Conversely, students who lack social-emotional skills struggle with managing themselves, their relationships, and their school work. Ironically, children who are labeled *at-risk* have the highest need for SEC, but frequently are placed in environments where SEC is neither taught nor valued as an effective means for managing challenging behaviors. More importantly, at-risk students often find themselves in institutions where the adult-child or teacher-student relationship takes a lower priority to discipline and academics. Yet, according to research, teacher-student conflict is associated with negative feelings about school and decreases self-directedness and cooperation in the classroom. The result of this conflict is disengagement, defiance, lack of motivation, and absenteeism that ultimately impedes a child's academic success.

Of note, researchers suggest that early racial and income differences in the quality of teacher-student relationships may contribute to disparities in achievement (Pianta, Rimm-Kauffman, & Cox, 1999; Pianta & Walsh, 1996). These researchers have found that positive relations with teachers in the classroom and between home and school are less common for low-income students as well as African American and Latino students than for higher income, white students. The implications are far-reaching; if SEC is a leading predictor in academic achievement, and its very foundation is relational, then the problem of closing the achievement gap may require more emphasis on the development of strong teacher-student bonds.

Central to Mariposa's training is the cultivation of a *helping relationship*. Our unique approach is based on the works of Dr. Louise Guerney, Dr. John Gottman, and Dr. Ross Greene. Each asserts that attempts to change behavior are rarely effective unless a child feels understood. Therefore, Mariposa emphasizes the cultivation of a strong adult-child relationship when attempting to re-direct a child's behavior. A trusting relationship is key to fostering social-emotional competence in children.

**Introduction to the Course**
**Promoting Social-Emotional Competence: Managing Behaviors and Improving Performance** trains educators in how to increase social-emotional competence in children, including interpersonal and learning-related social skills, and in how to reduce problem behaviors by applying Mariposa's skills-based method. You will learn the basic concepts of social-emotional competence, the research-proven intellectual basis for Mariposa's approach to promoting SEC in students, and the framework for applying Mariposa's approach. Building on this foundation, you will be trained how to apply these skills to real-world situations.

This course is designed for Pre-K through Grade 12 teachers of any subject who seek to address challenging classroom behaviors, improve the overall classroom climate, and increase student engagement and motivation to learn. The course involves extensive coaching in the practical application of program content to your work environment. You will be immersed in 16 hours of in-class presentations, role-play demonstrations, hands-on skills practice, and group discussions. Outside individual preparation and collaborative work is expected to run on the order of another 16 hours.

## Course Organization

The course will begin with a review of the theory and research linking social-emotional competence, academic achievement, and classroom behaviors. Subsequent sections will be dedicated to teaching and practicing the five key skills. Each skills section includes a definition of the skill, an overview of the research linking the use of that skill in pursuing specific learning-related outcomes, and a review of the steps to implement that skill. Skill sections also include numerous examples of typical ineffective ways that adults try to change a student behavior or motivate a child and contrast these with effective skilled interventions. Role-play demonstrations further reinforce the use of the skill to provide realistic examples. Instructors will also provide guidance and feedback during the skills practice exercises designed to address common behavior problems in the classroom.

The second component of the professional development – individual and collaborative work – will involve: (a) developing and implementing an action plan to address a challenging relationship with an individual student, (b) developing and implementing an action plan to engage other adults in support of the student, (c) developing and implementing a plan to address a problem behavior on a classroom-wide level, and (d) participate in a journaling process to enhance personal and professional insight into the processes introduced throughout the course.

# Section 1: Orientation

# Section 1: Orientation

**Section Objectives**

- Identify overall objectives and outline section topics
- Describe course requirements including assignments and attendance policy
- Examine conventional approaches to challenging behaviors and compare them to the Mariposa model
- Define social-emotional competence
- Identify the five essential skills to building social-emotional competence in children

# Section Outline and Course Objectives

This companion guide accompanies Mariposa's course, **Promoting Social-Emotional Competence: Managing Behaviors and Improving Performance**, and includes eight separate lessons, or sections:

    Section 1: Orientation
    Section 2: Social-Emotional Competence
    Section 3: Empathy
    Section 4: Personal Message
    Section 5: Cooperative Problem Solving
    Section 6: Descriptive Reinforcement
    Section 7: Inductive Discipline
    Section 8: Fostering Systemic Change

By the end of this class, you will achieve the following key learning objectives:

- Understand the core concepts behind social-emotional competence and the skills required to foster social-emotional competence

- Understand the Mariposa Method, which centers on five key skills for reducing behavior problems and improving the quality of teacher-student relationships as well as teacher-parent relationships

- Demonstrate competence in the Mariposa Method by applying it to two real-time interpersonal situations, one challenging behavior involving student and the other challenging behavior involving a classroom-wide issue

- Apply the skills to engage other adults (e.g., parents, teachers, therapists) in support of the student

- Develop self-awareness by using a journaling process throughout the course to reflect upon your application of the skills

**Course Requirements**

*Attendance*

Attendance is mandatory. However, we recognize that there are times when illness or other conflicts may occur. If it is absolutely necessary to miss a class, please contact the instructor in advance of the class and coordinate time to make up the missed material.

*Reading*

The course requires the use of two books:
- Greene, R.W. (2009). *Lost at school: Why our kids with behavioral challenges are falling through the cracks and how we can help them.* (1st ed.). New York: Scribner.

- Gottman, J. (1997). *Raising an emotionally intelligent child.* New York: Simon & Schuster.

In addition to the required reading, we strongly recommend that you read two additional titles at some point:
- Dweck, C.S. (2008). *Mindset: The new psychology of success.* New York: Random House.

- Zins, J.E., Weissberg, R.P., Wang, M.C., & Walberg, H.J. (Eds.). (2004). *Building academic success on social and emotional learning: What does the research say?* New York: Teachers College Press.

*Assignments*

Participants are asked to complete weekly reading and journal assignments based on class content. In addition, through a process of weekly assignments that build on each other, participants will develop an action plan to address a particular student's challenging behavior ultimately enhance that student's support from other adults as well. Participants will also complete an assignment intended to address a classroom-wide behavior problem with their students, and write a course summary paper intended to encourage reflection upon the overall impact of the course on their strategies and goals moving forward.

## Kids Do Well If They Can

> *Helping kids with social, emotional, and behavioral challenges is not a mechanical exercise. Kids aren't robots, adults aren't robots, and helping them work together isn't robotic. The work is hard, messy, uncomfortable, and requires teamwork, patience, and tenacity, especially as the work involves questioning conventional wisdom and practices.*
> (Greene, 2008, p. xi)

### Introduction to Challenging Behaviors

In our work with teachers, the issues of student engagement and managing challenging behaviors appear at the top of the *Need Support* list. And national surveys name behavioral issues as the number one challenge facing teachers. Yet teachers receive very little training on ways to address children's emotional and behavior problems. And teachers know that the persistence of challenging behaviors in classrooms and among students imposes upon valuable instruction time and works against student engagement.

Most response efforts to challenging behaviors have largely centered on behavior modification protocols or zero-tolerance policies, which in the long term do very little to develop lasting results. Why aren't they more effective? *Because they lack a connection to the causes of challenging behavior.*

### Our Explanations Guide Our Interventions

Part of the obstacle blocking adult effectiveness as it relates to challenging behavior is a lack of understanding about what causes challenging behavior. This lack of understanding shows up in our perceptions, beliefs, and philosophies regarding why children exhibit negative or challenging behaviors. Too often our explanations for negative behaviors alienate us from children, making it nearly impossible to provide the guidance they need to shift such behaviors.

Mariposa's philosophy, borrowed from Greene, is "kids do well if they can." From the outset, then, *we* make the assumption that if a kid is acting out it is because he or she is lacking a particular social-emotional skill, and has not learned to get his or her needs met constructively.

Mariposa's explanation for negative behaviors: Challenging behaviors result when the demands of a situation exceed a child's social-emotional competence.

When they cannot respond adaptively, kids act out or in. Thus, it is helpful to first understand what skills are lacking, then help children develop the skills needed. Greene (2008), author of **Lost at School**, notes, "If you don't know what skills a kid is lacking, you won't possess a true understanding of his challenges"(p. 11). The Mariposa Method begins with the development of a helping relationship.

Let's take a look at three common perceptions about challenging behaviors and an alternative perception for each.

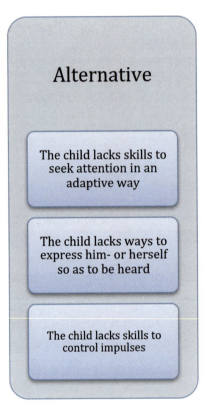

### A New Way of Seeing Challenging Behaviors: Lagging Skills and a Need to Build Social-Emotional Competence

When we are able to shift our beliefs and perspectives, and focus on a lagging skill versus a personality flaw, personal defect, or impossible family situation, then we can affect change and begin to develop social-emotional competence in children. Challenging behaviors present themselves as opportunities to deepen our relationships with children and teach them skills that will last a lifetime. The list below identifies characteristics exhibited when a specific social-emotional competency is missing. Though not a comprehensive list, it offers a new way of seeing into and understanding challenging behaviors, while underscoring the need for mentorship around social-emotional competence.

- **Lack of Self-Awareness** – Difficulty expressing concerns, needs, or thoughts in words
- **Lack of Social-Awareness** – Difficulty appreciating how one is coming across or being perceived by others; difficulty starting conversations, entering groups, connecting with people; difficulty with basic social skills
- **Lack of Responsible Decision Making** – Difficulty seeing the gray areas (i.e., black and white thinking); difficulty deviating from rules, routines
- **Lack of Relationship Skills** – Difficulty working cooperatively with peers or adults
- **Lack of Self-Management** – Difficulty handling transitions, shifting from one mind-set or task to another; difficulty considering the likely outcomes or consequences of actions (impulsive)

**Section Review**

1. What role do perceptions and beliefs play in shaping the way we respond to children and challenging behaviors?

2. How could your current explanations of challenging behavior affect the way you approach your relationships with children and adults?

3. How does the Mariposa Method differ from conventional approaches to addressing challenging behaviors?

# Social-Emotional Competence Assessment

## A Case Study / Action Plan in the Making

This course is designed to provide you, the Social-Emotional Coach, with opportunities to reflect upon the content and apply it in practical ways that are customized to suit your needs. It is our goal that you are able to first focus on one child with whom you may cultivate your skill set. To begin this process, you will need to complete the case study form below and be prepared to discuss its content during the next class.

---

**Basic Information**

Name of Child:                                      Age:

Grade (if applicable):                              Gender:

Race and/or Ethnicity:

---

For numbers 1-6, use another sheet of paper to answer. Remember, you do not need to answer every single question, but you do need to provide a full assessment of each of the questions in bold (1-4 sentences each). **This assessment will be the basis for a semester-long case study.**

1. **Describe this child and your relationship with this child.** Consider the following:
   - How does this child normally behave? What are some of his/her challenging behaviors? What are some of the contributing factors? What are some of his/her triggers?
   - How does this child relate to you? Describe the nature and quality of his/her relationship with you.

- What do you know about this child's family situation? How do his/her parents or other caregivers interact with him/her?

2. **Describe how this child relates to himself/herself.** How does he/she seem to view himself/herself? What does the child say or demonstrate about how he/she feels about himself/herself? How does this child express his/her emotions? (Self-Awareness)

3. **Describe how this child relates to others.** How does he/she respond to social situations? What kind of impact does this child have on his/her social environment, and conversely, what kind of impact does his/her social environment have on the child? (Social Awareness)

4. **Describe how this child responds to conflict and/or confounding situations.** What is this child's means of solving problems? How does this child typically respond to conflict? (Responsible Decision Making)

5. **Describe how this child responds to intellectual pursuits.** What is his/her level of engagement and motivation? What is this student's academic standing? What is his/her response to school? To education? (Relationship Skills)

6. **Describe this child's response to consequences.** How does this child make connections between behaviors and consequences? What attempts have been made to 'control' or 'contain' this child's behavior using consequences? (Self-Management)

# Section 2: Social-Emotional Competence

# Section 2: Introduction to Social-Emotional Competence

**Section Objectives**

- Identify the components of social-emotional competence and discuss key frameworks for organizing and understanding the underlying competencies.

- Describe the way that supportive teacher-student relationships affect student success.

- Identify the research linking social-emotional competence and the teacher-student relationship, student behaviors, emotional well-being, and academic achievement.

- Identify the skill that is the basis for helping relationships and fostering social-emotional competence.

# Social-Emotional Competence

*Because relationships and emotional processes affect how and what we learn, schools and families must effectively address these aspects of the educational process for the benefit of all students.* (CASEL, 2011, p. 405)

*Students typically do not learn alone but rather in collaboration with their teachers, in the company of their peers, and with the encouragement of their families. Emotions can facilitate or impede children's academic engagement, work ethic, commitment, and ultimate school success.* (CASEL, 2011, p. 405)

**Introduction to Social-Emotional Competence**
Schools play a pivotal role in raising healthy children who are both intellectually astute and who exhibit social-emotional competence. Teachers, in particular, are key to a child's development, acting as a constant influential presence *and* as the primary connection between home and school.

Teachers, students and the school as a whole are under immense pressure to perform. Student achievement is based on the results of high-stakes tests, as well as teacher pay and performance. Additionally, the success of the school measures tied to rates of expulsions and suspensions. Social-emotional competence benefits all involved in a school community, as supports understanding, empathy, and effective communication.

CASEL, a non-profit organization dedicated to advancing the research on social and emotional learning, defines social-emotional competence as **the ability to handle self and relationships as well as work effectively and ethically**. Further, the organization has translated these abilities into **comprehensible** categories, which are the basis for the Mariposa Method.

1. **Self-Awareness:** *The ability to assess one's feelings, interests, and strengths/weaknesses.* Children who are self-aware are better able to calm themselves in challenging situations, understand external and internal factors that trigger 'negative behaviors within themselves, and are able to communicate their feelings constructively.

2. **Social Awareness:** *The ability to understand another's point of view and understand social cues.* Social awareness is the basis for tolerance and respect. Children who are self-aware are able to work cooperatively with peers, make positive decisions that take into account the feelings, beliefs, and presence of others, and understand how their behavior affects a group.

3. **Responsible Decision Making:** *The ability to make ethical and effective decisions that consider the needs of others.* Children who make responsible decisions consider themselves and others as equally important, are able to look at a problem and come up with multiple solutions, weigh each outcome, and integrate ethics into the decision making process.

4. **Relationship Skills:** *The ability to create and maintain healthy relationships.* The quality of a relationship is determined by the respect given and received by the people involved. Children with **strong** relationship skills can navigate in and out of social situations, maintain friendships and thrive in adult-child interactions.

5. **Self-Management:** *The ability to monitor, evaluate, and modify emotional reactions* to accomplish one's goals. This skill is especially important when a child is facing a challenge, as it fosters impulse control, which leads to learning and long-term success.

## How Do We Foster SEC?

The Mariposa model has taken CASEL's categories one step further. We've delineated a relational method whereby each category is fostered by a specific communication technique, or one of Mariposa's 5 key skills.

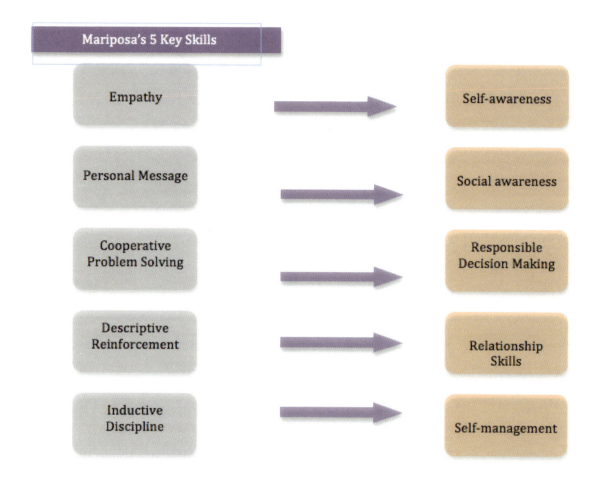

## Our Interactions with Children Shape the Way They Learn

It turns out that the way kids *feel* about school is often determined by the quality of relationships at their schools, which includes teacher-student *and* peer-to-peer relationships. Student perceptions of teachers' warmth and support, and of teachers as promoters of positive and respectful social interactions in the classroom, are significant predictors of student's academic motivation, engagement, and performance (Blum, McNeely, & Rinehard, 2000; Osterman, 2000; Ryan & Patrick, 2001).

Bryk and Schneider (2002) also found that the quality of social relationships operating in and around schools predicts positive student outcomes. So when it comes to academic achievement, student engagement, and healthy social interactions, a child's social-emotional competence or lack thereof contributes to each outcome.

> *Research proves that students who are emotionally connected to their peers, who have "bonded" with adults who value learning and expect high levels of academic performance, adopt the value of academic achievement and have a positive academic orientation.* (Hawkins et al., 1999; Learning First Alliance, 2001).

Once taken for granted as a natural developmental process, **we now know that deliberate, intentional, structured, and mindful interactions between adults and children can foster the development of social-emotional competence.** It is through and within relationships that children develop SEC- it is a reciprocal and dynamic process. By placing attention on the quality of the adult-child relationship and entering that relationship as an SEC coach, one begins to build the foundations of self-awareness, social awareness, responsible decision-making, healthy relationships, and self-management in kids.

## The Quality of Teacher-Student Relationships Matter

It has been well established that children's academic and social-emotional competencies, or lack thereof, are closely linked to the quality of their relationships with their teachers (Ladd, Birch, and Buhs 1999; Murray and Greenberg 2000). In fact, a national survey of adolescents revealed that the single most common factor associated with positive youth outcomes was a supportive relationship with an adult, and teachers were among the adults most frequently mentioned as the source of this support (Resnick et al. 1977). If positive connections to and interactions with children yield positive results, then we must also examine the relationship styles that produce counter effects. Since a relationship is not a static entity, we prefer to examine relationships through the lens of an interaction style. That is, the quality of a relationship is determined by its content and the ways in which people behave within its setting. We've categorized these interaction styles as follows:

- **Dismissive Interaction Style:** Here a child's emotions (particularly negative emotions) are disregarded, ignored, or trivialized. In classrooms where a teacher has a dismissive interaction style, kids may withdraw or act out because their needs are not being met. In addition, kids may be less likely to participate in class, less likely to take ownership of negative behaviors and their impact on the classroom environment, and more likely to engage in behaviors like name-calling, bullying, and teasing as 'emotions' are swept under the rug.

- **Disapproving Interaction Style:** With a disapproving interaction style, a child is criticized for displaying negative feelings and may be punished (shamed, reprimanded) for expressing emotion. When a child is shamed or reprimanded for expressing his or her emotion, he or she may internalize the judgments rendered by adults. In these classrooms, competitiveness and external validation are highly sought. The need to be 'good' trumps the need to be oneself and stunts the development of self-awareness and internal motivation.

- **Passive Interaction Style:** In the passive interaction style, a child's emotions are accepted and understood, but the child is not offered guidance or a framework (i.e., limits) on the child's behavior. Though expression is valued, limits and boundaries (i.e., mutual respect, problem solving, and even ethical behavior) are second to self-expression. In these classrooms, kids do not feel safe and often take it upon themselves to mete out justice as it relates to relational dynamics and/or test the limits and boundaries of the teacher and peers as well. Low expectations, both academic and behavioral, tend to shape this classroom culture.

- **Interaction Style of the Social-Emotional Coach:** In a social-emotional coaching style, an adult with an empathic ear listens to a child's emotions. Expression is valued, but also modeled and tempered by the cultivation of a 'helping' relationship between adult and child. In these classrooms, kids know the limits, boundaries, and expectations, yet they are encouraged and supported in the development of the self- and their relationships. A balance is struck between internal motivation and external feedback.

| Interaction Styles | Dismissive | Disapproving | Passive | Social-Emotional Coach |
|---|---|---|---|---|
| **Reaction to Emotions** | Treats child's feelings as trivial | Judges and criticizes child's expression of emotion | Embraces *all* emotional expression, but does not set limits and boundaries | Sees a child's emotions (positive or negative) as an entry point to building a helping relationship |
| **Internal Motivations** | May lack awareness of emotions in self or others | May be afraid of losing 'control' | May be afraid of intruding on child's sense of self | Is aware of the process of building a helping relationship; in tune with emotions and the lagging skills of the child; in tune with own emotions |
| **Attitudes & Beliefs** | May believe time will heal most problems; "Negative emotions are toxic!" | Believes negative emotions have a time limit; "Emotions need to be controlled, not expressed!" | Believes time will change how children express behaviors; "All you can do is ride it out!" | Believes emotions are valuable and essential to development; "Kids need support in expressing their emotions!" |
| **Effect on Classroom Environment** | Kids feel unsafe; creates an environment where name-calling, teasing, and bullying occur | Kids feel unsafe; creates a culture of shame and blame; kids motivated by external validation | Kids feel unsafe; creates an environment of low expectations | Kids feel safe; creates a healthy balance between self-expression and personal responsibility; Kids are taught how to problem solve, work cooperatively, and respect one another without excluding the self. |

## Section Review

1. Identify lagging social-emotional competence skills in a specific child and examine typical responses to their challenging behaviors.

2. What is social-emotional competence? What does the research say regarding its role in shaping student behaviors, contributing or detracting from academic success, and shaping school culture?

3. How does the quality of teacher-student and/or parent-child relationship relate to a child's ability to gain key social-emotional skills? Which kind of interaction style is most effective and why? Which are the least effective? Why?

4. Empathy as basis for building relationship– why should it come first?

# Handouts & Exercises
## Social-Emotional Competence

# *FOUR INTERACTION STYLES**
### *GOTTMAN, 1997*

## THE DISMISSING ADULT

**Beliefs**
- children's feelings are irrational, and therefore do not count
- negative emotions are harmful or toxic
- focusing on negative emotions will "just make matters worse"
- negative emotions mean the child is not well adjusted
- the child's negative emotions reflect badly on his/her parents

**Behaviors**
- treats child's feelings as unimportant and trivial
- disengages from or ignores the child's feelings
- wants the child's negative emotions to disappear quickly
- characteristically uses distraction to shut down child's emotions
- may ridicule or make light of a child's emotions
- shows little interest in what the child is trying to communicate
- may lack awareness of emotions in self and others
- feels uncomfortable, fearful, anxious, annoyed, hurt, or overwhelmed by the child's emotions
- fears being out-of-control emotionally
- sees the child's emotions as a demand to fix things
- minimizes the child's feelings, downplaying the events that led to the emotion
- does not problem-solve with the child
- believes that the passage to time will resolve most problems

**Effects of this style on children**: Children learn that their feelings are wrong, inappropriate, not valid. They may learn that there is something inherently wrong with them because of the way they feel. They may have difficulty regulating their own emotions.

---

## THE DISAPPROVING ADULT

**Beliefs**
- expression of negative emotions should be time-limited
- negative emotions need to be controlled
- negative emotions reflect bad character traits
- the child uses negative emotions to manipulate, which results in power struggles
- emotions make people weak; children must be emotionally tough for survival
- negative emotions are unproductive and a waste of time
- sees negative emotions (especially sadness) as a commodity that should be squandered

**Behaviors**

- displays many of the Dismissing Adult's behaviors, but in a more negative way
- judges and criticizes the child's emotional expression
- is over-aware of the need to set limits on their children
- emphasizes conformity to good standards or behavior
- reprimands, disciplines, or punishes the child for emotional expression, whether the child is misbehaving or not
- is concerned with the child's obedience to authority

**Effects of this style on children:** Same as the Disapproving style.

---

## THE LAISSEZ-FAIRE ADULT

### Beliefs
- believes there is little you can do about negative emotions other than to ride them out
- believes that managing negative emotions is a matter of hydraulics; release the emotion and the work is done

### Behaviors
- freely accepts all emotional expression from the child
- offers comfort to the child experiencing negative feelings
- offers little guidance on behavior
- does not teach the child about emotions
- is permissive; does not set limits
- does not help child solve problems
- does not teach problem-solving methods to the child

**Effects of this style on children:** Children do not learn to regulate their emotions; they have trouble concentrating, forming friendships, getting along with other children.

---

## THE SOCIAL-EMOTIONAL COACH

### Beliefs
- sees the world of negative emotions as an important arena for learning
- does not believe he or she has to fix every problem for the child
- is aware of and values his or her own emotions

### Behaviors
- values the child's negative emotions as an opportunity for intimacy
- can tolerate spending time with a sad, angry, or fearful child; does not become impatient with the emotion
- is sensitive to the child's emotional states, even when they are subtle
- is not confused or anxious about the child's emotional expression; knows what needs to be done
- respects the child's emotions
- does not poke fun at or make light of the child's negative feelings

- does not say how the child *should* feel
- uses emotional moments as a time to
    - listen to the child
    - empathize with soothing words and affection
    - help the child label the emotion he or she is feeling
    - offer guidance on regulating emotions
    - set limits and teach acceptable expression of emotions
    - teach problem-solving skills

**Effects of this style on children**: Children discover to trust their feelings, regulate their own emotions, and solve problems. They have high self-esteem, learn well, and get along well with others.

## Reflection Journal Questions

1. What is your most dominant interaction style based on the results of taking the Self-Test of Interaction Styles from Gottman? If Emotion Coach is your most dominant, which style received the second highest score?
2. Is there a difference between the way you interact at home and at school?
3. How does your upbringing influence your interaction style with children?
4. In looking at the five skills associated with the social-emotional coach, which skills come naturally to you and which skills do you anticipate being harder for you to implement? Why?

# Section 3: Empathy

# Empathy: Building Trust and Understanding

**Section Objectives**

- Define Empathy and describe the components that help to create an empathic statement.

- Describe the role that Empathy plays in developing a helping relationship.

- Identify the research linking Empathy with social-emotional competence and academic achievement.

- Recognize the specific learning-related, interpersonal skills, and competencies that are directly impacted by Empathy.

- Explain the role of Empathy in managing challenging behaviors.

- Apply Empathy as a first step to addressing a challenging behavior in a student.

# Section 3: Empathy – Building Trust and Understanding

*Ignoring the problem or not validating children's feelings hurts their ability to read the social situations. And, children will focus on a problem three times longer if they don't think that you understand their point of view.* (Beech, Berkenblit, Moore, & Roter, 2008, November)

*Empathy allows children to see their [teachers] as allies.* (Gottman, 1998, p. 73).

### Introduction to Empathy

Empathy is often misunderstood, especially when it involves interacting with children who display challenging behaviors. Our first impulse is to correct, redirect, or suggest, rather than listen attentively and act as a guide for a child. In this context, too, adults tend to equate Empathy with giving in to the demands of children or condoning negative attitudes and behaviors.

Mariposa sees and defines Empathy differently. For us, Empathy is a word with purpose: to achieve a clear understanding of a child's concern or perspective related to a given problem. It involves communicating understanding and acceptance of the feelings behind a child's words, actions, or point of view.

> Empathy: Communicating an understanding and acceptance of the feelings behind a child's words, actions, or point of view

Showing Empathy:

1. Enables a child to become aware of feelings he or she may not have recognized.
2. Gives children words for emotions, decreasing the need for them to act them out.
3. Fosters trust, the first step toward a helping relationship between adult and child.
4. Calms both the brain and body, making a child receptive to guidance, new information, and problem solving.
5. Increases the child's willingness to accept emotions in themselves and others.

The more that children begin to see and use language as a vehicle for expression, the less they will need to act out strong emotions in the form of challenging behaviors.

### The Mariposa Model of Empathy

Empathy involves three steps: **Listen** to the child's words while noticing body language and facial expression; **Identify** the child's feelings and point of view; **Communicate** acceptance and understanding of the child's perspective through an empathic statement.

**Listen**
- Listen without interruption
- Tune into the child's body language and facial expression

**Identify**
- Consider what the child may be thinking, feeling, wishing
- Don't rule out the possibility of two conflicting feelings or goals

**Communicate**
- Use easy starters: "You think _____." "You feel _____." "You wish _____." "Part of you wants _____, while part of you wants _____."

**Empathy Requires Adults to Put Aside Their Own Agendas**

Most adults concerned with nurturing children's development have cultivated a repertoire of responses to emotional expressions: to teach, to problem solve, or to reassure. In spite of these good intentions, these automated responses can unintentionally shut down or escalate the child's emotions and even harm the relationship by disrupting trust. There is a time and place for teaching, problem solving, and reassuring, and these are necessary skills. However, in order for these skills to be most effective, the child needs to first feel understood.

Example

> Ms. White, a middle school Assistant Principal in a challenging school, struggles with students' attendance to school.
>
> "Why didn't you come to school yesterday, Dylan?" asked Ms. White. "I had to help my mom watch my little sister because she was sick," said Dylan.
> **"Dylan, school should be your number one priority right now,"** Ms. White responds.
>
> This last response is an example of Ms. White's adult agenda. As soon as Dylan opened up, Ms. White responded with criticism. Empathy is not <u>approval</u> of negative feelings and/or behavior, but simply <u>acknowledgement</u> of the child's feelings and experience.

As a Social-Emotional Coach, you deliberately begin with a child's emotions. For that reason, we begin with the practice of Empathy. The word practice is intentional, because, generally speaking, Empathy is a foreign practice, especially as a consistent response to 'managing' kids and classrooms, and creating school culture.

That said, it is important to make distinctions between what Empathy is and is not. In this way, we begin to master the practice of Empathy.

| **FINE-TUNING EMPATHY** ||
|---|---|
| Empathy Is… | Empathy Is Not… |
| • Accepting the child's *emotion* <br><br> • Identifying the child's emotion <br><br> • Reflecting the child's emotions through an empathic statement <br><br> • Describing the emotion in a neutral manner <br><br> • Acknowledging the child's experience | • Accepting the child's *behavior* <br><br> • Asking about the emotion <br><br> • Reassuring or sympathizing <br><br> • Judging feelings and behaviors <br><br> • Suggesting what to do |

Frequently teachers tell us that they are too busy to stop and use Empathy. Lack of time is an indicator to postpone Empathy, because Empathy *requires* attention. How and when Empathy is used contributes to its effectiveness.

### Creating a Helping Relationship

When adults use Empathy, they create the foundation for a helping relationship with their student. A helping relationship is not one where the adult is constantly assisting the child on how to behave; rather, this type of relationship is a collaborative effort, a working alliance, and a process that teachers and kids work through together (Greene 2008).

**Keeping Kids Safe: Times to Postpone Empathy**

Greene defines the helping relationship as a relationship that "provide[s] kids with tools to become more effective self-helpers and more responsible agents of change in their own lives" (Greene 2008, p. 54). Empathy is the first step in shaping the helping relationship, however there are times when kids need adults to effectively communicate and address what is acceptable versus what is not. In these situations, we postpone Empathy. We developed the acronym STOP to help you remember.

| When to Postpone Empathy (S T O P) | |
|---|---|
| **S**afety! | When safety is at stake, it is best to postpone Empathy. For example, let's say you notice a child hit another child. First, make sure the child who was hit is okay and ensure that the child who hit has stopped. |
| **T**antrums or Tuning You Out! | Empathy has the ability to calm a raging or upset child. However, if a child is not able to hear, come back to Empathy when the child is able to listen. Note, the more time that we spend using Empathy proactively (or times when the emotional intensities are low) the less time you will be spending in times of crisis. |
| **O**bjectives | When a serious misbehavior has taken place, your objective may be to first communicate your disapproval of the act before exploring the feelings behind the child's actions. The former could send a confusing message to the child. |
| **P**ressed for Time | Imagine that the bell has rung, and kids are changing from 1st to 2nd period. As a kid leaves your room, he wells up in tears explaining that another child has been picking on him. You begin to panic, because your rowdy second period is piling into your classroom. Instead of using Empathy and risk sounding disinterested, postpone the Empathy. Instead, try something like this: *"It is important to me to talk with you more about this; you being treated poorly is upsetting to me. I would like to talk about this and now is not a good time because I have to begin. Let's talk about this at lunch today. I'll send someone over with a pass.* |

# In Summary

**Empathy** involves listening to the child and reflecting back exactly what they are saying to you in a manner that communicates understanding and acceptance of the feelings.

When adults use Empathy, they are communicating in a way that is free of judgments, criticisms, problem solving or adult agendas. This skill may seem simple, but it requires much practice.

Empathy fosters **self-awareness**. When adults give children the words that identify what they are feeling, children are more willing to accept emotions in themselves and others. This skill is the first step in building a trusting, helping relationship between adult and child.

**Empathy** has three steps: listen to the child, identify his or her feelings, and communicate those feelings back. Empathy never starts with "I."

**Section Review**
1. How does Empathy contribute to healthy relationships?
2. How does Empathy look, sound, and feel?
3. Why do adults typically skip over Empathy?
4. What do they do instead? And why?
5. Give an example of a typical teaching response that does not use Empathy, and adapt it to reflect Empathy instead.

# Handouts & Exercises
## Empathy

# Empathy

<u>Definition of Empathy</u>
Communicating an understanding and acceptance of the feelings behind a child's words, actions, or point of view; the ability to understand and label a child's emotions or underlying needs/motivation

<u>Mechanics of Empathy</u>
Empathy involves three steps:
1. Listening to the child's expressions
2. Identifying the child's feelings/point of view
3. Phrasing a statement that conveys acceptance and understanding of the child's feelings/point of view.

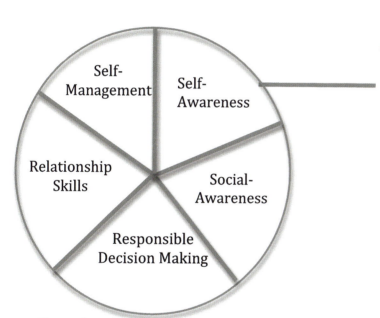

## Social Emotional Competence*

**Empathy** promotes social-emotional competence because it fosters *self-awareness.* In order to handle conflicts effectively, children must first be able to recognize when they are hurt or angry and then calm themselves. Children must first understand and accept their feelings and points of view before they are able to understand the feelings of others. When adults use empathy, children become more self-aware and are more likely to communicate their feelings constructively.

<u>Example:</u>
**Child's expression**: *"That dumb old teacher! She is always picking on me and I don't do anything."*
**Feelings/point of view:** Unfairness, anger, hurt
**Empathic response:** *"You think the teacher is being unfair and that really makes you mad."*

*Collaborative for Academic, Social and Emotional Learning (CASEL). (2009). *SEL: What is it and how does it contribute to students' academic success?* www.casel.org/pub/dvds.php#powerpoint, Slide 4.

## 15 Challenging Characters: Empathy Skills Practice

For each scenario below, form an empathic response to communicate that you understand and accept how the child feels. The following questions may help you gain a deeper understanding of the child's experience.

"If I were this child…"

◊ What would I be thinking about myself positively or negatively?

◊ What would I be feeling?

◊ What would I be wishing?

◊ What would I be thinking about doing?

◊ What conflicts might I be experiencing?

---

### Example

Negative Nancy tends to expect the worst.

**Child Statement:** *"Why should I even bother raising my hand– You never call on me."*

**Empathic Response:** *"You don't see the point of trying when you already know it is not going to work."*

---

1. Shy Shonda has sat alone for lunch for the past couple weeks. Noticing her sad face, you ask how she is doing.

   **Child Statement and/or Behavior**: *"I'm fine. I don't like those kids anyhow – my real friends are at my other school."*

   **Empathic Response:**


2. Hyperactive Harry is constantly getting out of his chair during class.

   **Child Statement and/or Behavior**: *"I need to sharpen my pencil. Can I just sharpen it really quickly?"*

   **Empathic Response:**

3. Picked-on Paul has repeatedly come back from recess complaining of being called names by the other children.

   **Child Statement and/or Behavior**: *"Tyrone keeps calling me a baby right in front of everyone!"*

   **Empathic Response:**

4. Even Steven thinks that you have it out for him. During math, you notice him nudge another classmate. When you address him about his behavior, he gets very defensive.

   **Child Statement and/or Behavior**: *"He did it first! How come you always punish me and do nothing to him?"*

   **Empathic Response:**

5. Impulsive Ira keeps getting in trouble for starting fights.

   **Child Statement and/or Behavior**: *"I won't hit anyone again, I promise."*

   **Empathic Response:**

6. Frustrated Fredericka has difficulty understanding math. During one of your lessons you notice that she is not participating. You walk over to her and inquire why she is not participating in the lesson.

   **Child Statement and/or Behavior**: (Staring out the window) *"I can't get any of these stupid math problems."*

   **Empathic Response:**

7. Lonely Laura is often left out during group activities in class.

   **Child Statement and/or Behavior**: *"No one wants me in their group— it is because I look weird!"*

   **Empathic Response:**

8. Comparing Carlos is continually sizing himself up against other classmates. After handing back the test from the previous day, you overhear him asking another student what he got on the exam.

   **Child Statement and/or Behavior:** *"I got all of the problems right! What grade did you get Joel?"*

   **Empathic Response:**

9. Uncertain Ursula has a hard time working independently. She frequently asks for feedback when working on a project even though you have communicated the importance of trying first, then asking if you get stuck.

   **Child Statement and/or Behavior:** *"Mr. Jones, I need some help. Is this right? Am I doing this the way I am supposed to?"*

   **Empathic Response:**

10. Anxious Amanda loves soccer but is concerned about this week's tryouts.

    **Child Statement and/or Behavior:** *"I don't want to try out. My stomach hurts."*

    **Empathic Response:**

11. You learn that a fight broke out in school. One child got beaten up while the others watched and did nothing. Bystander Billy saw what took place but is refusing to tell the name of the bully.

    **Child Statement and/or Behavior:** *"What am I supposed to do, be a snitch?"*

    **Empathic Response:**

12. Forgetful Felix has a hard time remembering to bring his homework folder back to school.

    **Child Statement and/or Behavior:** *"Please don't be mad at me – I forgot my folder again!"*

    **Empathic Response:**

13. Today after school is the school play and everyone is excited about it. Chatty Charlie and Talkative Tom are excessively talking about this in the back of your class. You interrupt class and nicely ask them to stop.

    **Child Statement and/or Behavior**: Both students acknowledge your comment with a nod. However, when you begin teaching they continue their conversation.

    **Empathic Response:**

14. Rigid Ralph is not happy about changes in seating.

    **Child Statement and/or Behavior**: *"What happened to my desk? Why can't I just sit where I was before?"*

    **Empathic Response:**

15. Distractible Dante has a hard time completing any assignments because he is distracted by other things going on in the classroom. You are constantly trying to encourage him to stay on track.

    **Child Statement and/or Behavior:** During your math lesson, you notice Dante staring out the window and playing with his pencil.

    **Empathic Response:**

# Case Study / Action Plan

## Empathy

Directions: Choose a student with whom you have a challenging relationship.

A. Please write a brief description of the situations in which the challenging behaviors occur.

_____

_____

B. List three challenging statements/behaviors of this student.

1. _____

2. _____

3. _____

C. Answer the following questions with this student in mind.

1. What would I be thinking (+) or (-) about myself in this situation?

   _____

2. What would I be feeling?

   _____

3. What would I be wishing?

   _____

4. What would I be thinking about doing?

   _____

*Promoting Social Emotional Competence: Managing Behaviors and Improving Performance*

5. What conflicts would I be experiencing?

   _____

D. Identify a time to have a conversation with this student.

E. Write out how you would open the conversation with your student.

   _____

   _____

F. Formulate three empathic responses to the student's three statements/behaviors above.

   1.

   _____

   2.

   _____

   3.

   _____

# Reflection Journal Questions
## Ideas for reflecting on the skill of Empathy

Before implementation of skill:

1. What challenges do you anticipate regarding the use of Empathy? What reservations do you have?

2. What is your typical response to challenging behaviors? With regard to the student from your case study, how do you typically address his/her challenging behaviors and emotions?

3. Greene talks about identifying the lagging skills in children as the key for fostering change. Thinking about yourself, what are your lagging skills? How do these help or hurt your ability to help challenging students?

After implementation of skill:

1. How did it go? How did the student respond? How did you respond?
2. What surprised you? What challenges arose? What successes did you have?
3. What questions or thoughts were you left thinking about?
4. Did you have any aha moments? Based on your experience, have you rethought any of the ideas below? If so, how?
    - Peer to peer relationships
    - Teacher-student relations
    - Parent-teacher relations
    - Classroom culture
    - School culture
    - Instruction
    - Other

# Section 4: Personal Message

# Section 4: Personal Message - Communicating Feelings and Expectations

**Section Objectives**

- Define Personal Message and describe the components that help to create a Personal Message.
- Describe the role that Personal Messages play in developing healthy relationships.
- Identify the research linking Personal Message with social-emotional competence and academic achievement.
- Recognize the specific learning-related, interpersonal skills, and competencies that are directly impacted by Personal Message.
- Explain the role of Personal Message in reducing challenging behaviors.
- Apply Personal Message as a second step to addressing a challenging behavior in a student.

# Personal Message - Communicating Feelings and Expectations

*The healthy child sees his person as separate from his acts. A sense of personal value independent of behavior is essential to his self-esteem. How you talk to children affects whether they make the vital distinction between behavior and self.* (Briggs, 1988, p. 57)

**Introduction to The Personal Message**

As teachers, we want children to know and understand how their behavior affects others and their environment. While most children are able to label their behavior as 'good' or 'bad', few are aware of the impact their behavior has on others.

Relaying a Personal Message communicates the affects of their behavior to children, develops Empathy, and fosters social awareness.

So, what is the Personal Message? It is a series of authentic statements that communicates your feelings and thoughts about a child's behavior in a constructive yet *real* way.

> Personal Message: Communication of one's own needs and feelings in a manner that is respectful and most likely to be heard or understood; communicating your feelings and thoughts about a child's behavior in this manner helps children see things from your perspective.

**The Mariposa Model of The Personal Message**

Children need to hear personal reactions from adults and others to keep their behavior within bounds. Typically, when a child misbehaves, we redirect him or her by telling the child what they did wrong and what they should have done. We often omit how their behaviors made us feel and how it personally affected us. The Personal Message includes both the emotion and personal impact. Remember, the following steps can be reversed:

## State

| State your feelings. Start with an "I" statement. | "I feel angry..." |

⬇

## Describe

| Describe the child's behavior and how it made you feel | "I feel angry when you call me names." |

> Note: in some cases, you may want to **identify** what you want the child to do instead after your personal message.
> "I would like you to call me by my real name."

When you are transparent about your emotions and provide *specific* feedback about a child's behavior, you aid in the child's development of social awareness. The child is able to hear how you feel, empathize with you, and relate to you as a person who has feelings, wants and aspirations. The child begins to understand that he/she is accountable for more than the self. This brings balance to the helping relationship and allows the child, at the very least, to consider the impact of his or her behaviors.

The third part in the Personal Message--identify what you want the child to do--teaches the child how to treat you, and in so doing, teaches him/her how to treat others. This step may be optional, depending on the situation. As SE coaches, we act as living examples to demonstrate quality relationships and the ethical treatment of persons. Even when we make 'mistakes' this teaches the child another aspect of *authentic, ethical* relations: compassion.

> In short, the personal message benefits children and adults alike:
> 1. **Gives the child meaningful feedback**
> 2. **Models constructive self expression**
> 3. **Helps the child understand your feelings**
> 4. **Gives the child a chance to take action on his or her own**
> 5. **Increases the likelihood that the child will hear what you have to say**
> 6. **Has a calming effect on the adult**

**Communicating a Personal Message Means...**

Honesty and self-reflection matters. Your ability to step out of the role of the all-knowing teacher and step into a relationship with students begins with the willingness and awareness of your current practices. Often obstacles block this path. Our feeling, beliefs, and personal perceptions influence our practice. When it comes to the Personal Message, a few pitfalls come to mind:

- Thinking your 'job' is to build the character of students
- Having an agenda and prescribed solution
- Being unaware of your own needs and boundaries
- Refusing to share your own needs and boundaries

Keeping these pitfalls in mind also helps us make distinctions between what a Personal Message is and what it is not.

### FINE-TUNING PERSONAL MESSAGE

| A Personal Message Is… | A Personal Message Is Not… |
|---|---|
| • Stating how a child's behavior makes you feel<br>• Expressing how a child's behavior affects you<br>• Expressing an outcome you want for the child | • Judgment of the child's behavior<br>• Problem solving for the child<br>• A time for consequences |

We are all social-emotional coaches in-training, working to find the most effective ways to develop meaningful relationships with students. We all want these relationships and the lessons learned therein to carry over into the next classroom, next grade, next school, and throughout a child's life.

Fostering social awareness begins with communicating in a manner that your message will be heard and understood – that is, with a Personal Message. Remember:

## In Summary

> **A personal message** involves communicating your feelings, thoughts, and needs about a child's behavior in a manner that is most likely to be heard and understood. It also identifies what you would like the child to do. And while it may seem simple, it takes practice to master.
>
> **A personal message** helps foster social awareness in children and it models constructive self-expression. Children are less likely to bully and be bullied when adults around them use personal messages because personal messages foster social awareness. This awareness builds when you provide feedback to children about how their behavior affects others, in this case, you. When you express your feelings in this manner you model constructive (assertive) self-expression to children.
>
> **A personal message** has two steps. State how you feel, identify the behaviors that made you feel that way, and if necessary, clarify what you want the other person to do.

**Section Review**

1. How does a Personal Message contribute to healthy relationships?
2. Why do Empathy and Personal Message go hand-in-hand?
3. Why do adults typically leave their feelings out when communicating with children?
4. What do they do instead? And why?
5. How much should an adult share with the child? When is sharing adult feelings too much?

# Handouts & Exercises

## Personal Message

**Personal Message Responses**

<u>Personal Message</u>: I (feel, want, wish, need…) because…

1. I am frustrated that you just dumped your pencils on the desk because it interrupted my lesson.

2. I am upset that you did not give this to me sooner, as I do not have enough time to help you on this project since that it is due tomorrow.

3. I am worried that you're not going to understand this math problem if you keep talking with your classmate.

4. I am disappointed that you have not taken care of the your classroom duties as you had said you would. I also resent having to do the job that you said you were going to do.

5. I am mad that you are writing on the desk. I wonder if you realize how much I care about keeping the classroom neat.

6. I am proud that you answered the questions even though you were scared your answer was wrong.

7. I get very frustrated when you continue interrupting my conversation. It is hard for me to concentrate when I have to stop what I am saying to talk to you.

8. I wish that you would be more careful when throwing that ball. I am worried that you are going to hurt your classmate.

9. I am glad that you seem better. I was worried that you might have continued feeling badly.

10. It is hard for me to read when you are horsing around with your friends.

11. I am very mad that you did not come when you said you would. I trusted that you would be in class when you said you would. Now you have missed your assignment.

12. I noticed that you offered Tom the chalk. I wish you had asked me before you did that.

13. It is important to me that you tell me the truth. I am disappointed that you told me you did not hit her when I saw that you did. I am also mad that you hit him. I wish that you could use your words and tell me why you are upset instead of hurting him.

14. I resent having to clean up what you said you were going to do. I feel taken advantage of when I let you do a fun class project and you do not help me by cleaning.

15. I am so glad that you both waited quietly like I had asked.

## Personal Message Handout

<u>Definition of Personal Message</u>
Communication of your own needs and feelings in a manner that is respectful and most likely to be heard or understood. Communicating feelings and thoughts about a child's behavior in this manner helps children see things from your perspective.

<u>Mechanics of Personal Message</u>
A Personal Message involves two steps:
1. Describe the child's behavior
2. State how you feel

> **Personal Messages** foster *social awareness*. In order to handle conflicts effectively, children must first be able to recognize when others are hurt or angry. Social awareness is the basis for tolerance and respect. When adults use Personal Messages, they model constructive self-expression and provide feedback on how a child's behavior affects others.

Promoting Social Emotional Competence: Managing Behaviors and Improving Performance

Example:

**Child's expression**: *"I hate doing homework. I don't understand why we need to learn this stuff."*

**Feelings/point of view (of yourself):** You want your student to enjoy learning; or you are worried or frustrated that he or she is not learning.

**Personal Message:** *"When you do not finish your homework, I get worried that you will fall behind. I would like you to complete all the items on your worksheet."*

**3 Important Points to Remember**

1. When stating your feelings, give the reason behind your feelings.

   > **Example:** "I'm very angry that you said you would clean up your table and you did not."

2. Let the child know that you have a problem with the child's behavior that accounts for the way you feel. (This is the key to getting the student to listen).

   > **Example:** "My head aches so badly, I'm afraid I won't be able to listen to your piano playing now. Please wait till later."

3. Don't condemn, accuse, or embarrass your children. These actions make them feel they have to defend themselves and distract them from hearing what you have to say.

   > **Example:** "I'm very angry that I cannot count on you for anything; you're so irresponsible."
   >
   > **Instead:** "I am angry because you did not do what you said you would do. Now we will not be ready on time."

*Collaborative for Academic, Social and Emotional Learning (CASEL). (2009). *SEL: What is it and how does it contribute to students' academic success?* www.casel.org/pub/dvds.php#powerpoint, Slide 4.

## 15 Challenging Characters: Personal Message Skills Practice

For each scenario below, form a Personal Message to communicate that you understand and accept how the student feels. The following questions may help you gain a deeper understanding of the student's experience:

"If I were this student…"

◊ What would I be thinking about myself positively or negatively?

◊ What would I be feeling?

◊ What would I be wishing?

◊ What would I be thinking about doing?

◊ What conflicts might I be experiencing?

---

**Example**

Negative Nancy tends to expect the worst.

**Student Statement:** *"Why should I even bother raising my hand? You never call on me."*

**Empathic Response:** *"You don't see the point of trying when you already know it is not going to work."*

**Personal Message:** *"I really value your input, Nancy. I was not aware that I was not calling on you as much as the other students."*

---

1. Shy Shonda has sat alone for lunch for the past couple of weeks. Noticing her sad face, you ask how she is doing.

   **Student Statement and/or Behavior**: *"I'm fine. I don't like those kids anyhow; my real friends are at my other school."*

   **Empathic Response:** *"Part of you would rather sit alone than have to sit with the other students." "You feel like these students aren't your real friends. Your true friends are back at your other school." "It is easier to be alone than to have to make new friends. "You feel like they already have their friends and it's hard to be the new girl."*

   **Personal Message:**

2. Hyperactive Harry is constantly getting out of his chair during class.

   **Student Statement and/or Behavior**: *"I need to sharpen my pencil. Can I just sharpen it really quickly?"*

   **Empathic Response**: *"It is hard to continue working when your pencil is not sharpened. When something is bothering you, it is very hard to sit still."*

   **Personal Message:**


3. Picked-on Paul has repeatedly come back from free time complaining of being called names by the other students.

   **Student Statement and/or Behavior**: *"Tyrone keeps calling me a baby right in front of everyone!"*

   **Empathic Response**: *"You want him to stop but he just keeps picking on you."*

   **Personal Message:**


4. Even Steven thinks that you have it out for him. During math, you notice him nudge another student. When you address him about his behavior, he gets very defensive.

   **Student Statement and/or Behavior**: *"He did it first! How come you always punish me and do nothing to him?"*

   **Empathic Response:** *"You feel like I have it out for you."*

   **Personal Message:**


5. Impulsive Ira keeps getting in trouble for starting fights with students from other classes.

   **Student Statement and/or Behavior**: *"I won't hit anyone again, I promise."*

   **Empathic Response**: *"This time you mean it."*

   **Personal Message:**

6. Frustrated Frederica has difficulty with math. During one of your lessons, you notice that she is not participating. You walk over to her and inquire why she is not participating in the lesson.

    **Student Statement and/or Behavior**: (Staring out the window) *"I can't get any of these stupid math problems. I wish I was at home."*

    **Empathic Response:** *"You are so discouraged and feel like giving up. You are also feeling homesick."*

    **Personal Message:**


7. Lonely Laura is often left out during group activities after school.

    **Student Statement and/or Behavior:** *"No one wants me in their group—it's because I look weird!"*

    **Empathic Response:** *"You think they don't want you in their group because of the way you look and that really hurts your feelings."*

    **Personal Message:**


8. Comparing Carlos is continually sizing himself up against other students. After handing back the test from the previous day, you overhear him asking another student what he got on the exam.

    **Student Statement and/or Behavior:** *"I got all of the problems right! What grade did you get, Joel?"*

    **Empathic Response:** *"You want to know if Joel did as well as you."*

    **Personal Message:**


9. Uncertain Ursula has a hard time working independently. She frequently asks for feedback when working on a project even though you have communicated the importance of trying first and then asking for help if she gets stuck.

    **Student Statement and/or Behavior:** *"Mr. Jones, I need some help. Is this right? Am I doing this the way I am supposed to?"*

    **Empathic Response:** *"You want some reassurance that you are on the right track."*

    **Personal Message:**

10. Anxious Amanda has a new Facebook page and is nervous about what the other students in her class will say to her. She's also nervous because she doesn't want any teachers to find out.

   **Student Statement and/or Behavior:** *"No, I don't have a Facebook page. And even if I did, the other students would just make fun on me."*

   **Empathic Response:** *"You are scared that you're going to get in trouble for having a Facebook page and you are also nervous about what other students might say about it."*

   **Personal Message:**


11. You learn that a fight broke out during recess. One student got beaten up badly while others watched and did nothing. Bystander Billy saw what took place but is refusing to tell the name of the bully.

   **Student Statement and/or Behavior:** *"What am I supposed to do, be a snitch?"*

   **Empathic Response:** *"You are torn, while you know we need you to tell us the name of the bully, you're worried that if you tell you could end up in the same boat as the victim."*

   **Personal Message:**


12. Forgetful Felix has a hard time remembering to record his homework assignments and then bring them in the next day.

   **Student Statement and/or Behavior:** *"Please don't be mad at me, I keep forgetting to study and I didn't take my homework planner home last night."*

   **Empathic Response:** *"You are trying to remember your materials but you just keep forgetting. It is very discouraging for you and you are worried you are in trouble."*

   **Personal Message:**


13. Today is the school play and everyone is excited about it. Chatty Charlie and Talkative Tom are excessively talking about this in the back of your class. You interrupt class and nicely ask them to stop.

   **Student Statement and/or Behavior:** Both students nod at your comment and then roll their eyes when you walk away. When you return your attention to the spelling bee, they continue their conversation, but more loudly this time.

**Empathic Response:** *"It is hard to stay quiet because you are more interested in your own conversation than my lesson."*

**Personal Message:**


14. Rigid Ralph is not happy about changes in seating.

    **Student Statement and/or Behavior:** *"What happened to my desk? Why can't I just sit where I was before?"*

    **Empathic Response:** *"You are concerned and confused because you do not know why you have to change your seat. You would prefer that I left you where you were."*

    **Personal Message:**


15. Distractible Dante has a hard time completing any assignments because he is distracted by other things going on in the classroom. You are constantly trying to encourage him to stay on track.

    **Student Statement and/or Behavior:** During work time, you notice Dante staring out the window and playing with his pencil.

    **Empathic Response:** *"It is hard to concentrate when there are other things going on outside and you have a lot on your mind."*

    **Personal Message:**

# Case Study/ Action Plan

## Personal Message

Directions: Please refer to the challenging situation identified in your homework for Empathy Case Study Action Plan.

A. Describe the problem behavior from your point of view.

_____

_____

_____

B. Answer the following questions with yourself in mind.

6. What do I think (+) or (-) about myself in response to this situation?

_____

7. What do I feel?

_____

8. What do I wish would happen?

_____

9. What am I thinking about doing?

_____

10. What conflicts am I experiencing?

_____

C. Identify three Personal Messages that you might communicate to your student.

1. _____

2. _____

3. _____

# Reflection Journal Questions

## Ideas for reflecting on the skill of Personal Message

Before implementation of skill:

1. What challenges or reservations do you have regarding using a Personal Message? How do you feel about sharing your feelings and wishes with the children you teach?
2. How is the Personal Message different from the way you typically convey how a child's behavior is affecting you or others?

After implementation of skill:

1. How did it go? How did the student respond? How did you respond?
2. What surprised you? What challenges arose? What successes did you have?
3. What questions or thoughts were you left thinking about?
4. Did you have any aha moments? Based on your experience, have you rethought any of the ideas below? If so, how?
    - Peer to peer relationships
    - Teacher-student relations
    - Parent-teacher relations
    - Classroom culture
    - School culture
    - Instruction
    - Other

# Section 5: Cooperative Problem Solving

# Section 5: Cooperative Problem Solving – Finding Solutions Together

**Section Objectives**

- Define Cooperative Problem Solving and list the corresponding steps.
- Describe the role that Cooperative Problem Solving plays in helping children learn to develop healthy relationships.
- Identify the research linking Cooperative Problem Solving to social-emotional competence and academic achievement.
- Recognize the specific learning-related, interpersonal skills, and competencies that are directly impacted by Cooperative Problem Solving.
- Explain the role of Cooperative Problem Solving in reducing challenging behaviors.
- Apply the Cooperative Problem Solving process toward the development of an action plan to address a specific issue/problem with a student.

# Cooperative Problem Solving – Finding Solutions Together

*Most difficult problems don't get solved in a nanosecond…Solving a difficulty durably requires reflection, consideration, time and a willingness to let the process of exploring solutions unfold without premature interruption* (Greene, 2010, p. 106)

*What's the definition of an ingenious solution? Any solution that is doable (by both parties), realistic, and mutually satisfactory. If a solution isn't doable, realistic, and mutually satisfactory, the problem isn't solved yet* (Greene, 2010, p. 108).

## Introduction to Cooperative Problem Solving

In classrooms bustling with kids, disputes and conflicts are bound to occur. In response, adults often make it their business to end disputes and squash conflicts *for* children. In this way, the adult becomes responsible for keeping the peace and problem solving for kids. For kids, it means never learning how to problem solve, and for adults it guarantees frustration. It also explains why kids seem to repeat the same behavior without understanding how or why it yields the same result.

> Cooperative Problem Solving: A process in which adults work *with* children to identify goals, dissect problems, and strategize for success.

## The Mariposa Model of Cooperative Problem Solving

Mariposa encourages Cooperative Problem Solving. It includes working together to identify mutually satisfying goals, anticipating obstacles ahead of time, and breaking down problems into manageable steps. Cooperative Problem Solving helps kids make responsible decisions, think through consequences ahead of time, and resolve social problems by considering everyone involved. It gives children the time and space to consider the impact their choices have on themselves and others. Here's how it works:

## STEPS

| Describe the Problem | Listen and identify the problem at hand. Use Empathy to get the best understanding of the problem from the child's view as well as describe the problem from your point of view.<br><br>Stay with this step until all concerns have been heard. |
|---|---|
| Identify the Goal | Identify the child and adult goals.<br><br>What do you want to have happen?<br><br>What does the child want?<br><br>Use Empathy and a Personal Message to reiterate the child's goals. |
| Brainstorm Solutions | Invite the child to problem solve with you.<br><br>Before giving your ideas, ask the child if he/she has any ideas.<br><br>Consider writing all of the ideas down on a sheet of paper. |
| Evaluate Options | Support the child by thinking together about the outcome of each solution.<br><br>Refer back to goals to consider the best solutions. |
| Choose a Plan | After weighing options and goals, select a plan. |
| Touch Back | Pick a day or time to check in with the child to see how things are going.<br><br>If plan needs to be altered, guide the child through the steps again. |

**Empathy and Personal Message are the Foundation**

Dr. Ross Greene (2010) says that Cooperative Problem Solving "helps adults clarify and understand a child's concerns about or perspective on a particular unsolved problem…[It] also helps the kid understand the adult's concerns about the problem" (p. 53). Greene is talking about the first two skills: Empathy and

Personal Message. These two skills are integral to the problem solving process because of their ability to create a foundation of a helping relationship. And a helping relationship's purpose is to assist children in managing a problem at hand and prevent problems from occurring at all.

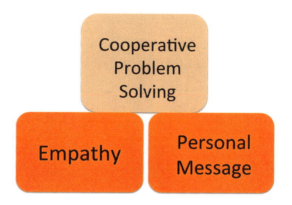

**The Benefits of Cooperative Problem Solving**
- Encourages cooperation and responsible behavior
- Contributes to learning
- Provides predictability
- Reduces stress and anxiety for both teacher and student
- Helps with discipline
- Encourages openness and collaboration between child and adult

**Tips for Implementation**

It's important to remember your role and goals as a Social-Emotional Coach. As a guide whose ultimate purpose is to model effective ways to solve problems, in this case, it is important to walk the child through each step and refrain from solving problems for them. **Give the child an opportunity to use his or her logic, intuition, and value system in choosing what works best for him or her.** What may be the most viable solution for an adult may not be the best solution for a child.

> *"The child needs to become convinced that you're just as invested in making sure his concern gets addressed as you are in making sure yours gets addressed"* (Greene, p. 82).

When brainstorming solutions *remember to remain non-judgmental*. Allow the child to come up with an array of solutions, even if you know the solutions will fail. Here's why. When you and the child move to the next step—evaluate options—you'll think through each solution, weigh its effect, and match it to a personal goal. A solution that is not mutually satisfying will lose, hands down. Allowing the child to process in this way shows him or her how to consider the consequences of a particular choice and recognize its misalignment with personal goals. This is a powerful lesson for children. And the practice enables a child to value the process, and thus begin to develop the ability to cope with challenges autonomously.

Finally, remember to touch back. Real solutions take time, effort, and sometimes trial and error. Touching back teaches children to evaluate the quality of choices made and adjust if necessary. It helps them develop realistic expectations of themselves and others. And, it helps understand that problem solving can be complex.

## In Summary

> **Cooperative Problem Solving fosters responsible decision-making.** It involves describing problems from all perspectives and working together to create mutually satisfying goals. And children are less likely to exhibit challenging behaviors when the adults around them use Cooperative Problem Solving.
>
> **Cooperative Problem Solving involves effective solutions that are mutually satisfying.** To be successful, solutions must meet the needs of the adult and the child.
>
> *Note: Take notice of triggers and try to be proactive about Cooperative Problem Solving. (i.e., lunch with student, during student conferences). Try to use Cooperative Problem Solving in instances that do not require immediacy and conflict resolution that is not pressing.*

**Section Review**

1. How does Cooperative Problem Solving contribute to healthy relationships?
2. How do the first two steps in Cooperative Problem Solving incorporate Empathy and Personal Message?
3. Give an example of a time when you (or a colleague) has gotten into a power struggle with a student. Consider how Cooperative Problem Solving might have shifted the dynamic to allow for the creation of an enduring solution.
4. What is the difference between Dr. Ross Greene's "collaborative problem solving" and Mariposa's Cooperative Problem Solving?
5. Explain why Cooperative Problem Solving improves executive functioning, decreases power struggles, and promotes teamwork.

# Handouts & Exercises

## Cooperative Problem Solving

## Cooperative Problem Solving
## Idea Sheet

| Steps | Conversation Starters | Tips |
|---|---|---|
| **Describe the problem** | *I notice that…* | Make sure to describe from all perspectives. |
| **Identify goals** | *What do you want to have happen?* | Invite the child to problem solve. Do not forget to clarify what you would like to have happen. |
| **Brainstorm solutions** | *What do you think might help?* | Hold off evaluating until you have at least 2 ideas from your student. |
| **Evaluate options** | *How do you think that would go? What if…* | Remember to anticipate obstacles. |
| **Choose a Plan** | *Moving forward…* | Be sure to clearly identify all aspects of the plan. |
| **Touch Back** | *Lets touch base again on Wednesday…* | Choosing a specific time and location will be helpful. |

*Promoting Social Emotional Competence: Managing Behaviors and Improving Performance*

## 15 Challenging Characters: Cooperative Problem Solving Skills Practice

For each scenario below, use the 6 steps of Cooperative Problem Solving to determine a plan of action that is mutually satisfying and realistic. Please consider these steps involved in creating a Cooperative Problem Solving when creating your plan.

1. **Describe the problem from all perspectives** *(I notice that…")*
2. **Identify goals** *("What do you want to happen?")*
3. **Brainstorm solutions** *("What do you think might help?")*
4. **Evaluate options** *("How do you think that might work?")*
5. **Choose the most effective plan** *("Moving forward, the plan will be…")*
6. **Touch back** *("Let's touch base next week to see how things are working.")*

---

**Example:** Negative Nancy tends to expect the worst.

**Child Statement:** *"Why should I even bother raising my hand? You never call on me."*

**Empathic Response:** *"You don't see the point of trying when you already know it is not going to work."*

**Personal Message:** *"I really value your input, Nancy. I was not aware that I was not calling on you as much as the other students."*

Cooperative Problem Solving:
1. *"I notice that you are not raising your hand as much as usual. What's up?"*
2. *"I would like to help you learn ways to think more positively, even when you feel like there is no use in trying. Do you have any suggestions?"*
3. *"Do you have any suggestions?"* (2 from student and 2 from adult)
    a. Nancy could make a list of all the things that she is grateful for and turn these in at the end of the day.
    b. Nancy could keep a journal to become more aware of her thoughts.
    c. Nancy could make a list of behaviors she avoids as a result of expecting the worse and try at least two per day.
4. Nancy might not keep up with a journal. Nancy may make a list of things she will try, but may need the teacher to see this so that she can monitor her efforts. She may not have time during school to do this.
5. *"Moving forward, you will use the first five minutes of study hall each afternoon to write down your thoughts. If these are negative, reframe them into positive expectations (hopes/wishes). If these are some behaviors that you have been avoiding, identify them and try at least one of them tomorrow."*
6. *"I will check your ideas briefly after study hall and then again at the end of the week so we can discuss how this is working."*

For Steps 1-3 in each question, follow the first three steps in Cooperative Problem Solving. For Step 4 in each question, choose a plan and describe why you chose the mutually satisfying solutions.

1. Shy Shonda has sat alone at lunch for the past couple weeks. Noticing her sad face, you ask how she is doing.

    **Child Statement and/or Behavior**: *"I'm fine. I don't like them anyhow; my real friends are at my other school."*

    **Empathic Response:** *"Part of you would rather sit alone than have to sit with students who are not your true friends."… "It is easier to be alone than to have to make new friends."… "You feel like they already have their friends and it's hard to be the new girl."*

    **Personal Message:** *"It's important to me that you feel welcome and included here. Even though it is not your old school, I hope that you will come to like it here."*

    **Cooperative Problem Solving:**
    1.
    2.
    3. *"Do you have any ideas?"*
        1.
        2.
        3.
    4.

2. Hyperactive Harry is constantly getting out of his chair.

    **Child Statement and/or Behavior:** *"I need to sharpen my pencil. Can I just sharpen it really quickly?"*

    **Empathic Response**: *"It is hard to continue working when your pencil is not sharpened. When something is bothering you, it is very hard to sit still."*

    **Personal Message:** *"It is hard for me to teach the class when you keep getting out of your chair."*

    **Cooperative Problem Solving:**
    1.
    2.
    3. *"Do you have any ideas?"*
        1.
        2.
        3.
    4.

3. Picked-on Paul has repeatedly come back from recess complaining of being called names by the other children.

   **Child Statement and/or Behavior**: *"Tyrone keeps calling me a baby right in front of everyone!"*

   **Empathic Response**: *"You want him to stop but he just keeps picking on you."*

   **Personal Message**: *"I am angry that he is treating you like that. I want to help figure out a way to put an end to this."*

   **Cooperative Problem Solving:**
   1.
   2.
   3. *"Do you have any ideas?"*
        1.
        2.
        3.
   4.

4. Even Steven thinks that you have it out for him. During math you notice him nudge another classmate. When you address him about his behavior, he gets very defensive.

   **Child Statement and/or Behavior**: *"He did it first! How come you always punish me and do nothing to him?"*

   **Empathic Response**: *"You feel like I have it out for you."*

   **Personal Message**: *"I don't want to make you feel like I have it out for you. I am just frustrated and not sure what to do to get you and the others to stop disrupting the class."*

   **Cooperative Problem Solving:**
   1.
   2.
   3. *"Do you have any ideas?"*
        1.
        2.
        3.
   4.

5. Impulsive Isaac keeps getting in trouble for starting fights.

   **Child Statement and/or Behavior**: *"I won't hit anyone again, I promise."*

   **Empathic Response**: *"This time you mean it."*

   **Personal Message**: *"I am very frustrated that this keeps happening and am not sure what to do to help you."*

   **Cooperative Problem Solving:**
   1.
   2.
   3. *"Do you have any ideas?"*
       1.
       2.
       3.
   4.

6. Frustrated Frederica has difficulty understanding math. During one of your lessons you notice that she is not participating. You walk over to her and inquire why she is not participating in the lesson.

   **Child Statement and/or Behavior**: (Staring out the window) *"I can't get any of these stupid math problems."*

   **Empathic Response**: *"You are so discouraged and feel like giving up."*

   **Personal Message**: *"I want to make this less frustrating for you and I am wondering what I can do to help."*

   **Cooperative Problem Solving:**
   1.
   2.
   3. *"Do you have any ideas?"*
       1.
       2.
       3.
   4.

Promoting Social Emotional Competence: Managing Behaviors and Improving Performance

7. Lonely Laura is often left out.

   **Child Statement and/or Behavior:** *"No one wants me in their group with me, it's because I look weird!"*

   **Empathic Response:** *"You think they don't want you in their group because of the way you look and that really hurts your feelings."*

   **Personal Messages:** *"I do not think that that is why you are not in a group. I wish you could see all the beauty that I see in you."*

   **Cooperative Problem Solving:**

       1.

       2.

       3. *"Do you have any ideas?"*

           1.

           2.

           3.

       4.

8. Comparing Carlos is continually sizing himself up against other classmates. After handing back the test from the previous day, you overhear him asking another student what he got on the exam.

   **Child Statement and/or Behavior:** *"I got all of the problems right! What grade did you get, Joel?"*

   **Empathic Response:** *"You want to know if Joel did as well as you did."*

   **Personal Message:** *"It is important to me that my students support one another. Telling Joel that you got them all right and then asking him what he got is not being supportive. Next time please refrain from comparing you grades with others."*

   **Cooperative Problem Solving:**

       1.

       2.

       3. *"Do you have any ideas?"*

           1.

           2.

           3.

       4.

9. Uncertain Ursula has a hard time working independently. She frequently asks for feedback when working on a project even though you have communicated the importance of trying first, then asking if you get stuck.

   **Child Statement and/or Behavior:** *"Mr. Jones, I need some help. Is this right? Am I doing this the way I am supposed to?"*

   **Empathic Response:** *"You want some reassurance that you are on the right track."*

   **Personal Message:** *"I get annoyed when you ask for help when I asked you to give the problem a try before asking for my help."*

   **Cooperative Problem Solving:**
   1.
   2.
   3. *"Do you have any ideas?"*
       1.
       2.
       3.
   4.

10. Anxious Amanda loves soccer but is concerned about this week's tryouts.

    **Child Statement and/or Behavior:** *"I don't want to try out. My stomach hurts."*

    **Empathic Response:** *"You are nervous about tryouts and do not want to go."*

    **Personal Message:** *"I don't want you to miss out on an activity you might really enjoy because you are nervous. On the other hand, I do not want to force you to play if you really don't want to."*

    **Cooperative Problem Solving:**
    1.
    2.
    3. *"Do you have any ideas?"*
        1.
        2.
        3.
    4.

11. You learn that a fight broke out during recess. One child got beaten up while the others watched and did nothing. Bystander Billy saw what took place but is refusing to tell the name of the bully.

    **Child Statement and/or Behavior:** *"What am I supposed to do, be a snitch?"*

    **Empathic Response:** *"You are torn, while you know we need you to tell us the name of the bully, you're worried that if you tell you could end up in the same boat as the victim."*

    **Personal Message:** *"I am so upset that this happened and want to make certain that it doesn't happen again. I wish that children who stood watching would have felt empowered to take action."*

    **Cooperative Problem Solving:**
    1.
    2.
    3. *"Do you have any ideas?"*
        1.
        2.
        3.
    4.

12. Forgetful Felix has a hard time remembering to bring his homework folder back to school.

    **Child Statement and/or Behavior:** *"Please don't be mad at me—I forgot my binder again!"*

    **Empathic Response:** *"You are trying to remember your folder but you just keep forgetting. It is very discouraging for you and you are worried you are in trouble."*

    **Personal Message:** *"It is frustrating for me that you forget your homework because I want you to be able to participate in class."*

    **Cooperative Problem Solving:**
    1.
    2.
    3. *"Do you have any ideas?"*
        1.
        2.
        3.
    4.

13. Today is the school play and everyone is excited about it. Chatty Cathy and Talkative Terry are talking about this in the back of your class. You interrupt class and nicely ask them to stop.

   **Child Statement and/or Behavior**: Both students acknowledge your comment with a nod. However, when you begin teaching they continue their conversation.

   **Empathic Response:** *"It is hard to stay quiet because you are so excited about the school play."*

   **Personal Message:** *"It is very hard for me to finish the lesson when there is so much talking. It is very frustrating for me because I've already asked you to be quiet many times."*

   **Cooperative Problem Solving:**

       *1.*

       *2.*

       *3. "Do you have any ideas?"*

           *1.*

           *2.*

           *3.*

       *4.*

14. Rigid Ralph is not happy about changes in seating.

   **Child Statement and/or Behavior**: *"What happened to my desk? Why can't I just sit where I was before?"*

   **Empathic Response:** *"You are concerned and confused because you do not know why you have to change your seat. You would prefer that I left you where you were."*

   **Personal Message:** *"I would like to give every student a chance to work from all different seats in the room and with different students. I will work to help you adjust to your new arrangement."*

   **Cooperative Problem Solving:**

       *1.*

       *2.*

       *3. "Do you have any ideas?"*

           *1.*

           *2.*

           *3.*

       *4.*

15. Distractible Dante has a hard time completing any assignments because other things going on in the classroom distract him. You constantly are trying to encourage him to stay on track.

    **Child Statement and/or Behavior:** During your math lesson, you notice Dante staring out the window and playing with his pencil.

    **Empathic Response:** *"It is hard to concentrate on school work when there are other things going on in the classroom and outside."*

    **Personal Message:** *"I want to help you to finish an assignment without stopping or being distracted."*

    **Cooperative Problem Solving:**

    1.

    2.

    3. *"Do you have any ideas?"*

        1.

        2.

        3.

    4.

# Building a Community of Support: Planning for Your Meeting

## Cooperative Problem Solving

**Before the meeting**
1. **Identify at least one supportive adult in the child's life**. And, identify at least one educator or school personnel who is equally supportive of the child and the process.
2. **Before 'hosting' the meeting, set the purpose and tone.** You may do this in the form of a letter or a personal phone call. Briefly discuss the approach you've been using, consider mentioning SEC, and mention the value of partnering with parents and families in an effort to create a community of support around a child.

**During the meeting**
1. During the day of the meeting, reiterate the above before formally beginning the meeting.
2. Once the purpose has been set, give some background information on your relationship with the student. **Discuss what you and the child have been working on**. *Consider inviting the child to talk about his/her relationship to you. (Be sure to have a conversation with the child beforehand so he/she knows what to expect.)
   - I've known Tyrone since.
   - I first met Nadia when… and what I most remember about her…
   - I noticed during lunch Tyrone tended to ignore the lunch attendee…
   - I noticed Nadia was becoming increasingly disinterested in her Language Arts work.
3. **Walk the team through some of the conversations you and the child have had, noting what the feelings associated with the behavior:**
   - Tyrone seemed to be feeling, _____. We talked about it and he confirmed _____. He also added _____. Tyrone, would you add anything else? (Involve the child in the summary of your conversations)

- First, Nadia and I tried to talk about it during class, but she seemed to be shutting down. So we decided on talking during lunch. Right, Nadia?

4. **Talk about the core of the problem:** (begin with what was learned during Empathy)
   - Tyrone expressed he felt like he was being picked on. He felt disrespected when the lunch aid corrected him in front of his peers. He also felt disrespected by the lunch aid's tone of voice, which he described as loud.
   - Nadia expressed that she was feeling helpless, because even though she turned in all of her work, her grade remained at a B. She said she felt discouraged because the girls at her table all made a grade higher than her on the last project and she felt she deserved a high grade as well. She said, she was giving up because it didn't matter.
5. **Talk about your response:** (summarize your Personal Message/s to the child)
   - I told Tyrone that I want him to be comfortable in his surroundings and feel valued.
   - I told Nadia that I felt disheartened by her discouragement, and I wished she would continue her efforts in my class because she is one of my best students.
6. **Walk through the Cooperative Problem Solving steps:** (Cooperative Problem Solving)
   - Tyrone and I considered a few options and narrowed it down to three…
   - Nadia and I thought together about ways to resolve the situation. We came up with one solution…
7. **Invite the support of the team:** We wanted to invite you into the process. And talk about ways we can support _____ around this.
8. **Engage in the Cooperative Problem Solving with Team or with parents.** Be sure to include a touch back date.

### After the Meeting
1. Touch back in with team.
2. If needed, schedule another meeting to engage in Cooperative Problem Solving.

# Case Study / Action Plan

## Cooperative Problem Solving

*(In order to prepare for your meeting, please answer the following questions):*

1. Identify the time and place where this meeting will take place:
*"I would like to identify a time when you and I can meet to talk about..."*

_____

2. Describe how you will open the conversation:
*"I scheduled this meeting because I'd like to discuss..."*

_____

3. Write out your Empathy statement:

_____

_____

4. Write out your Personal Message:

_____

_____

_____

---

Directions: Apply the 6 Cooperative Problem Solving steps to address a challenging situation with your student.

1. **Describe the problem from all perspectives** *(I notice that...")*
2. **Identify goals** *("What do you want to happen?")*
3. **BrainStorm Solutions** *("What do you think might help?")*
4. **Evaluate options** *("How do you think that might work?")*
5. **Choose the most effective plan** *("Moving forward, the plan will be...")*
6. **Pick a time to Touch back** *("Lets meet again on Thursday to see how things went...")*

*Then use the Cooperative Problem Solving steps to conduct your meeting:*

1. Describe the problem:

2. Identify goals:

3. Identify 3 potential solutions:

4. Evaluate options:

5. Choose the most effective plan:

6. Identify a time when you will touch back:

# Reflection Journal Questions

## Ideas for reflecting on the skill of Cooperative Problem Solving

### Before implementation of skill:

1. What challenges or reservations do you have regarding Cooperative Problem Solving? How do you feel about allowing children to brainstorm solutions to problems? Where might you have the most difficulty in implementation? Why?
2. How are problems typically solved in your classroom? In your school? How are kids typically *taught* to solve problems in your school environment? (Both implicitly and explicitly)
3. How do you feel about allowing students to brainstorm solutions? Are you concerned with giving them some control? Are you concerned with time constraints in the classroom?

### After implementation of skill:

1. How did it go? How did the student respond? How did you respond?
2. What surprised you? What challenges arose? What successes did you have?
3. What questions or thoughts were you left thinking about?
4. Did you have any aha moments? Based on your experience, have you rethought any of the ideas below? If so, how?
    - Peer to peer relationships
    - Teacher-student relations
    - Parent-teacher relations
    - Classroom culture
    - School culture
    - Instruction
    - Other

# Section 6: Descriptive Reinforcement

# Section 6: Descriptive Reinforcement – Fostering Internal Motivation

**Section Objectives**

- Define Descriptive Reinforcement and the underlying components.
- Describe the role that Descriptive Reinforcement plays in helping children learn to develop healthy relationships.
- Identify the research linking Descriptive Reinforcement to social-emotional competence and academic achievement.
- Recognize the specific learning-related, interpersonal skills, and competencies that are directly impacted by Descriptive Reinforcement.
- Explain the role of Descriptive Reinforcement in reducing challenging behaviors.
- Apply the Descriptive Reinforcement process to build on the action plan being developed to address a specific issue/problem with a student

# Descriptive Reinforcement: Fostering Internal Motivation

*The most reliable factor leading people to change – by far – is the relationship they have with the person helping them change.* (Greene, 2008, p. 54).

## Introduction to Descriptive Reinforcement

Less than a decade ago, educators replaced phrases like *Good job!* or *Needs improvement*, with explicit narratives. *Good job* was replaced with, "I see you've used an engaging lead to begin your essay" or "You used the quickest methods to solve this equation, so maximized both your time and effort." *Needs improvement* was altered in a similar way, with phrases like "You need to raise your hand when speaking." With this shift, kids could see how their effort and/or behaviors contributed a particular outcome.

> **Descriptive Reinforcement:** Describing a child's actions and efforts and explaining their relevance to social emotional skills to increase desired behaviors.

Descriptive Reinforcement follows a similar modicum. Rather than labeling a child's behavior good or bad, adults can offer clear, constructive statements that *describe* a child's actions and efforts to increase desired behaviors. For example, let's say a child befriends a classmate who is being ostracized on the playground. We could pat the child on the back and say 'good job' or we could affirm the child's behavior in the following manner: "You saw that Lela was being left out and offered to be her friend. You risked being left out yourself. That takes courage." The first response is a simple judgment that offers external validation to the child. The second is a true witnessing and noticing of the child's behavior and the adult's response supports the child's internal motivation and encourages the continuation of that kind of behavior.

## The Mariposa Model of Descriptive Reinforcement

Descriptive Reinforcement fosters pro-social relationship skills. This type of communication provides children with the feedback they need to develop relationships that are respectful, supportive, and healthy. Here's how it works:

| Describe | |
|---|---|
| Describe what the child did as opposed to what they did not do. Be specific. | Instead of: "You didn't hit Marcel." Try: "You kept your hands to yourself." |

⬇

| Identify | |
|---|---|
| Identify the strength of this behavior and/or how the behavior affected you. | "That took a lot of self-control." Or "I am relieved because I was worried that he would be hurt." |

**Tips for Successful Implementation**

*How* we reinforce and what we choose to reinforce affects children's motivation and influences their assessment of themselves. The word 'reinforce' indicates that we are *again (re)* trying to remind a child of his or her efforts so that he or she can *in*ternalize the behavior, without needing external incentives. Adults need only use Descriptive Reinforcement when 'reminding' is needed. That which comes naturally to a child does not need to be reinforced:

| Refrain | Extend |
|---|---|
| •Does something out of self-interest (playing an instrument or reading)<br>•Is being creative (drawing or coloring)<br>•Is intently concentrating<br>•Is being rewarded naturally | •Is not interested in learning new behaviors (e.g., chores or manners)<br>•Is frustrated (e.g., trying to be kind to their peers but getting no response)<br>•Lacks self-control/discipline (e.g., transitions between lunch/recess)<br>•Is working to overcome a bad habit: (e.g., calling out in class |

*Promoting Social Emotional Competence: Managing Behaviors and Improving Performance*

**Descriptive Reinforcement Over Praise**

With good intentions, teachers often encourage students through praise. Yet, we've found that Descriptive Reinforcement fosters internal motivation and supports social-emotional competence. Praise, when used as the primary way to motivate and encourage students, creates dependency and causes children to seek external validation.

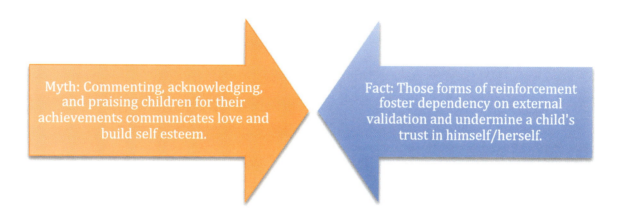

We want children to determine the quality of their actions, words, and choices based on their internal motivation. Instead of telling a child, "Good job!" try saying something that reinforces and/or affirms the behavior that pleases you rather than offering a judgment. For example, "You helped her feel included by asking her to sit at your table." We want children to make positive choices when no one's looking. By identifying a specific behavior and its impact on the self and others, you support a child's understanding of positive relationship building.

**Observe Rather than Judge**

In some ways, Descriptive Reinforcement feels counterintuitive because we've been conditioned to judge rather than observe. Though Descriptive Reinforcement can be challenging initially, it will pay off in the end. It will support children in developing healthy attitudes and behaviors toward themselves and others. And, as a Social-Emotional Coach it will change the way you see children and their behaviors. As we've seen and experienced throughout this course, true change begins with shifts in perception.

**Descriptive Reinforcement and Mindset**

In her book, *Mindset,* author Carol Dweck presents her research and findings on two mindsets: fixed versus growth. Throughout her book she provides examples of why we need to describe effort rather than praise an ability or talent. She brings the point home with many examples of successful people who have learned that effort and practice are needed to develop abilities and skills, and that failures and obstacles can actually inform future success. She then provides examples of famous people for whom an obstacle or failure has turned into a downward spiral because they believe their abilities are fixed and therefore beyond their ability to change. Characteristics of the two mindsets include:

| Fixed Mindset | Growth Mindset |
| --- | --- |
| • We are born with abilities and talents<br>• Our successes "prove" our abilities and talents<br>• Our failures bring our abilities and talents into question<br>• Challenges are frightening and to be avoided | • We can develop abilities and talents through hard work and practice<br>• Our successes are the result of hard work and effort<br>• Our failures help us learn, thereby giving us opportunities to improve<br>• Challenges are tools to hone our skills and to be pursued |

Dweck's research highlights the reason that it is important to praise process and effort rather than talent or intelligence: as children and adults, we have control over the amount of effort we put into a task or project, but how many people feel they have control over an ability that is essentially someone else's judgment of us? Descriptive Reinforcement focuses on specific behaviors that can be repeated or modified based on the feedback from adults, rather than making students feel judged as worthy or unworthy of acknowledgment.

# In Summary

> **Descriptive Reinforcement fosters relationship skills.** Descriptive reinforcement fosters pro-social relationship skills. This type of communication provides children with the feedback they need to develop relationships that are respectful, supportive, and healthy.
>
> **Descriptive Reinforcement** varies from praise and involves describing the behavior instead of labeling or judging.
>
> There are many times when **Descriptive Reinforcement** is not necessary, such as when a child is concentrating, being creative or is being naturally reinforcement. On the other hand, the time to extend reinforcement is when a child is overcoming a bad habit, is frustrated or lack self-control.

**Section Review**
1. How does Descriptive Reinforcement contribute to the development of healthy relationships?
2. What does it look like, sound like, and feel like?
3. When should you extend Descriptive Reinforcement and why? When should you refrain and why?
4. Explain why it leads to improved student motivation, pro-social behavior, engagement, and frustration tolerance.
5. What did you find challenging about Descriptive Reinforcement? Why?

# Handouts & Exercises

## Descriptive Reinforcement

## Praise vs. Encouragement

|  | **Praise** | **Encouragement** |
|---|---|---|
| Dictionary Definition | 1. To express a favorable judgment<br>2. To glorify, especially by attribution of perfection<br>3. An expression of approval | 1. To inspire with courage<br>2. To spur on/stimulate |
| Recognizes | Only complete, perfect product | Effort and improvement |
| Attitude | Patronizing, manipulative | Respectful, appreciative |
| "I" message | Judgmental: "I like the way you are sitting." | Self disclosing: "I appreciate your cooperation." |
| Used most often with: | Children: "You are such a good girl." | Adults: "Thanks for helping." |
| Examples | "I'm proud of you for getting an A in math." (robs person of ownership of own achievement) | "That reflects your hard work." (recognizes ownership and responsibility for achievement) |
| Invites | People to change for others | People to change for themselves |
| Teaches | What to think | How to think |
| Goal | Conformity: "You did it right." | Understanding: "What do you think/feel/learn?" |
| Effects on self-esteem | Feel worthwhile only when others approve | Feel worthwhile without the approval of others |
| Long-range effects | Dependence on others | Self-confidence, self-reliance |

# 15 Challenging Characters: Descriptive Reinforcement Skills Practice

For each scenario or statement below, use Descriptive Reinforcement to describe the student's accomplishment.

| Example |
|---|
| Nancy has been raising her hand more in class. <br><br> **Descriptive Reinforcement:** *"I notice that you have been taking more chances in class."* |

1. Shonda has been more assertive lately. Today she approached some students and asked them if she could join them for lunch.

   **Descriptive Reinforcement:**

2. Harry has stayed in his chair throughout the entire lesson.

   **Descriptive Reinforcement:**

3. Paul has managed to find other students to spend time with during free time. As a result, Paul was not picked on by the usual kids.

   **Descriptive Reinforcement:**

4. You notice that Steven is following the directions this week without upset or outrage. He's even smiled at you a few times.

   **Descriptive Reinforcement:**

5. Isaac has managed to refrain from starting fights, in spite of the fact that students have been picking on him to try and start fights.

   **Descriptive Reinforcement:**

6. During math, Frederica has come to you for help instead of giving up on her math assignment.

   **Descriptive Reinforcement:**

7. Laura has been more focused on her talents by putting energy into her art project after school. She is less focused on the actions of others and more focused on herself.

   **Descriptive Reinforcement:**

8. After handing back this week's quiz, Carlos refrains from asking other students how they did.

   **Descriptive Reinforcement:**

9. Ursula finished her assignment without asking you or her peers for help or feedback.

   **Descriptive Reinforcement:**

10. Amanda is reaching out to make new friends instead of talking about missing her friends at her old school.

    **Descriptive Reinforcement:**

11. Billy stood up to the bullying student and told you who beat up the other student earlier this week.

    **Descriptive Reinforcement:**

12. Felix remembered to take his homework folder and agenda home and return them to school the next day.

   **Descriptive Reinforcement:**

13. Cathy and Terry refrained from talking during the remainder of the spelling bee.

   **Descriptive Reinforcement:**

14. Ralph decided to try working with a new lab partner without being asked.

   **Descriptive Reinforcement:**

15. Dante has finished his homework on time.

   **Descriptive Reinforcement:**

# Case Study / Action Plan
## Descriptive Reinforcement

Directions: Apply the two Descriptive Reinforcement steps to address a challenging situation with your student:
1. Describe the expectation positively (in behavioral terms)
2. Identify words of Descriptive Reinforcement

If appropriate, identify an additional way to reinforce the desired behavior.


**I.** Identify three behaviors you would like to increase. State them positively and specifically and define them in behavioral terms.
**Example:** *"Use words that are appropriate and respectful"* as opposed to *"Don't disrespect me"* or a more general statement such as, *"Be good."*

1.

2.

3.

**II.** Identify words of Descriptive Reinforcement to be used when this student demonstrates the desired behaviors. Be sure to describe the behaviors as opposed to labeling the behavior as good or bad.
**Example:** *"You remembered to hold the door open for your friend."* This is preferable to a more general statement that casts judgment, like, *"Great job!"* or *"Good boy!"*

1.

2.

3.

**III.** If appropriate, identify how you would reinforce this behavior (e.g., observation, attention, affection, special treat/prize).

**Example:** On several occasions your student has cleaned up the art area without being asked. You decide to make him/her line leader to and from art.

1.

2.

3.

# Developing an Action Plan
## For Your Classroom

Before you begin solving the problems in your classroom, you need to identify the factors contributing to the misbehavior. Remember: *Challenging behaviors occur when the demands of a situation exceed the child's ability to respond adaptively.*

Check off the top 3 behavior problems you see in your classroom.

COMMON CLASSROOM PROBLEMS

__ Difficulty handling transitions, staying on task
__ Lack of respect for other students, teacher, and learning
__ Lack of engagement, motivation and/or attendance
__ Difficulty understanding directions and comprehending material
__ Lack of insight and/or concern for the consequences to their actions
__ Difficulty handling negative emotions when faced with an obstacle (social or learning-related); often leads to violence or confrontation
__ Bullying
__ Lack of self-control; students often getting out of chairs, asking to leave classroom and talking during lessons
__ Other _____

DEMANDS
Choose top classroom problem to answer.

When does this occur? What time of day? During which classes?
_____
_____

What are some triggers for this classroom behavior? Are there certain kids initiating this classroom-wide behavior?
_____
_____

Do you have other insights as to why this is common in your classroom? What other factors precede this problem? Certain dynamics?
_____
_____

*Promoting Social Emotional Competence: Managing Behaviors and Improving Performance*

What are the lagging skills behind this behavior? (See Greene pg. 287 for suggestions)

_____

_____

PROBLEM SOLVING

> Use the 6 steps to strategize a challenging situation with your whole class.
>
> - **Describe the problem from all perspectives** *(I notice that...")*
> - **Invite the class to problem solve** *("What do you want to happen?")*
> - **Brainstorm solutions** *("What do you think might help?")*
> - **Anticipate obstacles** *("How do you think that might work?")*
> - **Choose the most effective plan** *("Moving forward, the plan will be...")*
> - **Touch back**

1. Describe the problem:

_____

_____

1. Identify your goal/invite the class to problem solve:

_____

_____

3. Identify three potential solutions:

_____

_____

4. Anticipate obstacles:

_____

_____

5. Choose the most effective plan.

6. Plan a time to touch back to see if it worked or needs to be revised.

# Reflection Journal Questions

## Ideas for reflecting on the skill of Descriptive Reinforcement

Before implementation of skill:

1. How do you typically motivate students? Which strategies do you use? What has been its impact?

2. How do you feel about Descriptive Reinforcement as a strategy? What reservations do you have or what challenges do you anticipate?

After implementation of skill:
1. How did it go? How did the student respond? How did you respond?
2. What surprised you? What challenges arose? What successes did you have?
3. What questions or thoughts were you left thinking about?
4. Did you have any aha moments? Based on your experience, have you rethought any of the ideas below? If so, how?

- Peer to peer relationships
- Teacher-student relations
- Parent-teacher relations
- Classroom culture
- School culture
- Instruction
- Other

# Section 7: Inductive Discipline

# Section 7: Inductive Discipline - A Skill that Fosters Self-Management

**Section Objectives**

- Define Inductive Discipline and list the steps.
- Describe the role that Inductive Discipline plays in helping children learn to develop healthy relationships.
- Identify the research linking Inductive Discipline to social-emotional competence and academic achievement.
- Recognize the specific learning-related, interpersonal skills, and competencies that are directly impacted by Inductive Discipline.
- Explain the role of Inductive Discipline in reducing challenging behaviors.
- Apply Inductive Discipline to address a specific issue/problem with a student

# Inductive Discipline: A Skill that Fosters Self-Management

*[Social-Emotional Coaches] do set limits...and give their children clear and consistent messages about what behavior is appropriate and what behavior is not. When children know the rules and understand the consequences for breaking them, they are less likely to misbehave.* (Gottman, 1997, p. 67)

## Introduction to Inductive Discipline

Typically, our approach to discipline has been to use rewards and consequences or punishment to manage misbehavior. Yet, the benefits of each address problems in the short term, but often fall short as a long-term solution. You find yourself 'policing' children's behavior or having to repeat yourself continuously to get kids to listen.

Ultimately, we discipline children because we want them to exhibit self-control and self-responsibility. We want them to make choices that keep themselves and others safe. We've found that Inductive Discipline – stating rules and expectations in behavioral terms and identifying logical consequences – is an effective way to teach children to self-manage and take responsibility for their actions.

> Inductive Discipline: A form of discipline where adults state clear, consistent rules and expectations in behavioral terms and identifying logical consequences

Stating the rules sets clear expectations for children. Logical consequences allow children to connect behaviors to outcomes. Unlike punishment, logical consequences authentically link the behavior to the consequence, increasing the likelihood that the behavior modification will stick.

## The Mariposa Model of Inductive Discipline

The term Inductive Discipline is commonly used by psychologists to refer to the most effective type of adult discipline of children. Adults who use Inductive Discipline listen to children, but are also consistent in their enforcement of important rules and expectations.

Here's how it works:

## Describe

| Describe the behavior | "You are calling out during the midle of the lesson." |

⬇

## State

| State the rule or expectation positively. (Tell the child what he/she did as opposed to did not do.) | "When I am teaching, you must wait until I have finished speaking, then raise your hand and wait for me to call on you." |

⬇

## Warn

| Give a warning if the child breaks the rule again. Explain what will happen if the rule or limit is broken again. | "The next time you interrupt me, I will not respond to you until after our class discussion" |

⬇

## Implement

| If the child continues to break the rule, implement the consequence--what you explained would happen if the rule or limit was broken again. | "You have interrupted me again, _____ ." |

## Tips for Successful Implementation

It is extremely important for adults to <u>not</u> link the limit and the consequence. This diminishes the value of the limit, and also insinuates that the adult thinks that the child is not going to follow the limit in the first place. Rather, adults should describe the behavior and state the limit. Once the child does not follow the limit stated, then the adult can name the consequence.

It's important to state rules, limits, or expectations in clear, concrete behavioral terms. Being specific and consistent is vital, as you want the child to understand what is expected of him or her. Tell kids *what* to do rather than *what not* to do.

When choosing a consequence, it should be appropriate to the situation or behavior. The consequences you choose and the severity affects the likelihood that the rule will be followed and that learning will occur.

Keep in mind these guidelines when choosing consequences:
- **Severity**: The consequence should only be as severe as necessary to enforce the rule or limit.
- **Connection**: The consequence should be closely (or naturally) connected with the behavior.
- **Timing**: The consequence should follow as soon as possible after the rule or limit has been broken.

## Choose an adult-imposed consequence when:
- Emotional safety is in jeopardy
- Physical safety is in jeopardy
- Protection of valuable property is in jeopardy
- When the natural consequence is not strong enough to change behavior

## Inductive Discipline Applies Consequences that Reinforce Learning

A consequence is a negative experience that occurs as a result of a broken limit. There are three categories of consequences, and each has a relationship with specific rules/expectations. A consequence should be logically related to the behavior.

- A **natural consequence** teaches the child a lesson without the adult getting involved.
- A **logical consequence** has a direct connection with the broken limit.
- An **unrelated consequence** does not have a direct connection with the broken limit.

## Natural Consequences

- If a child is late for school, it goes on his/her record.
- If a child does not do his homework, he/she might do poorly on an exam.

## Logical Consequences

- If a child throws trash on the floor, then he/she must clean it up.
- If child is disturbing his/her peer, during an assembly, then the child's seat is moved.

## Unrelated Consequences

- If a child fights at school, the child loses recess privileges for a week.
- If a child does not turn in homework, he/she cannot turn in classwork.

Inductive Discipline fosters self-management. Children develop self-control when their world is organized and predictable. Children internalize reasonable rules of conduct and their rationales, and come to use these principles in their own decision-making process. When children know what to expect, things are less unknown and scary. This gives them the feeling of more control, which can lead to greater cooperation. Research has shown that children raised in this type of environment tend to have better self-regulation later in childhood and adolescence than children whose parents do not utilize Inductive Discipline. Though teachers are not parents, the same skills can be used to nurture a child's independence and growth in the classroom.

## In Summary

> **Inductive Discipline involves stating rules/expectations in positive behavioral terms and holding everyone accountable.** It involves identifying appropriate consequences ahead of time.
>
> **Inductive Discipline fosters self-management.** Children are less likely to present challenging behavior when adults use Inductive Discipline because Inductive Discipline fosters self-management.
>
> **Inductive Discipline has four steps:** Describe the behavior, state the rule or expectation, give a warning, and implement a consequence. The process seems simple, but requires practice to master.
>
> **Inductive Discipline requires that consequences be closely connected with the behavior.** You learned three categories of consequences—natural, logical, and unrelated—and learned how to choose the appropriate kind of consequence and when and how

**Section Review**
1. How does Inductive Discipline contribute to healthy relationships?
2. What are the steps? Why is it important to separate the limits from the consequences initially?
3. When is an adult-imposed consequence necessary?
4. Explain how Inductive Discipline fosters self-control.
5. How does Inductive Discipline differ from the disciplinary methods you have learned or experienced growing up?

# Handouts
## Inductive Discipline

### 15 Challenging Characters: Inductive Discipline Skills Practice

Following each negative communication:
   A. **Positively** state the behavior you would like to see happen.
   B. Determine whether a rule is necessary (Y/N).
   C. If Y, identify the consequence that will be imposed if the student is unable to follow the rule.

---
**Example**
Nancy is being disrespectful to another student's idea.
**Child Statement:** *"That is so stupid. It will never work."*
**Negative Communication:** *"That is disrespectful. Do not criticize other student's ideas."*
a) *"When you disagree with another student, voice your opinion in a more constructive and respectful manner."*
b) Y
c) Rephrase her comment using respectful language. *"For example, you might have asked, 'How would that idea work?'"*

---

1) Shonda refuses to welcome the new student.

**Child Statement:** *"I don't care about the new student. Why should I go over there and say hi?"*

**Negative Communication:** *"It is not very nice to ignore the new student."*
   a)
   b)
   c)

2) Harry gets up from his desk and proceeds to knock over the classroom display.

**Negative Communication:** *"How many times do I have to tell you to sit in your chair?"*
   a)
   b)
   c)

3) Paul runs up to you after lunch and says that all the children were picking on him again.

**Negative Communication:** *"You shouldn't be a tattle-tale, Paul."*
   a)
   b)
   c)


4) Even Steven takes another student's pencil without asking. When you reprimand him, he gets defensive.

**Child Statement:** *"I don't have a pencil! How come you always punish me for no reason?"*

**Negative Communication:** *"Do not talk back to the teacher."*
   a)
   b)
   c)


5) Isaac throws another child on the ground claiming they took his ball without asking.

**Child Statement:** *"That thief stole my ball!"*

**Negative Communication:** *"Just because he took your ball does not mean that you can hit him!"*
   a)
   b)
   c)


6) Frederika copies another student's answers during a math quiz.

**Negative Communication:** *"Cheating is taken very seriously here."*
   a)
   b)
   c)


7) Laura lashes out by crying and stomping her feet because she was left out of group activities yet again.

**Child Statement**: *"I hate it here! I just want to go home!"*

**Negative Communication:** *"We do not throw a temper tantrum when things don't go our way."*
   a)
   b)

c)

8) You overhear Carlos making fun of another student's athletic ability.

**Child Statement**: *"I don't think he could kick that ball over 3 feet!"*

**Negative Communication:** *"Do not make fun of other children."*

   a)

   b)

   c)

9) During an important test, Ursula raises her hand to ask for help. After you help her with one problem, she raises her hand again for help on the next problem.

**Negative Communication:** *"Do not ask me for help before you try the problem on your own. I will not always be here to help you."*

   a)

   b)

   c)

10) Amanda fakes having a headache and asks to go to the nurse in order to avoid gym class.

**Negative Communication:** *"It is not right to pretend that you are sick when you really are fine."*

   a)

   b)

   c)

11) Billy harasses another student out of fear of being ostracized.

**Child Statement:** *"Look at his big ears! He looks like Dumbo!"*

**Negative Communication:** *"Do not make fun of other children."*

   a)

   b)

   c)

12) Felix forgets to do his daily classroom chore, erasing the chalkboard, once again.

**Negative Communication:** *"If you don't start remembering to erase the chalkboard, I will give the chore to someone else."*

   a)

   b)

   c)

13) Charlie talked to Tom throughout the guest speaker's lecture.

**Negative Communication:** *"We don't speak when others are speaking."*

    a)

    b)

    c)

14) Ralph throws a tantrum when he has to work with a new partner in science class.

**Child Statement:** *"This is so stupid! I like my old partner better!"*

**Negative Communication:** *"Ralph, when I assign something, you do what I say."*

    a)

    b)

    c)

15) After assigning a handout 45 minutes ago, you realize that Dante has not even looked at it yet. He is too busy staring out the window at the cars passing by.

**Negative Communication**: *"Dante, why didn't you start your handout yet? You are wasting time!"*

    a)

    b)

    c)

# Restating the Rules

For each negative rule or expectation, restate in positive behavioral terms.

|  | RULE/LIMIT | RE-STATE RULE/LIMIT POSITIVELY |
|---|---|---|
| Example | No running in the hallways. | Students must walk in the hallways. |
| 1 | No hitting. | |
| 2 | No interrupting. | |
| 3 | No cheating. | |
| 4 | Do not steal other people's property. | |
| 5 | Do not damage other's property. | |
| 6 | Do not exclude or ignore others. | |
| 7 | Do not name call. | |
| 8 | No lying. | |
| 9 | Do not disturb other students when they are working. | |
| 10 | Do not disturb the teacher when they are helping another student or teaching a lesson. | |
| **Additional Examples** | | |
| | Do not talk behind other peoples' backs. | |

*Promoting Social Emotional Competence: Managing Behaviors and Improving Performance*

# Case Study / Action Plan
## Inductive Discipline

For each item below, please answer the following questions.

Identify a behavior you would like to change.
D. Positively identify the rule/limit (e.g., what you would like to have happen).
E. Determine whether a consequence is necessary (Y/N).
F. If Y, identify the consequence that will be imposed if the child is unable to follow the rule.

1. Behavior:

A. _____

B. _____

C. _____

2. Behavior:

A. _____

B. _____

C. _____

# Reflection Journal Questions

## Ideas for reflecting on the skill of Inductive Discipline

Before implementation of skill:

1. What is your definition of discipline? What is your school's definition of discipline?
2. How do you typically discipline students? What are your thoughts and feelings about Inductive Discipline? Your reservations?

After implementation of skill:
1. How did it go? How did the student respond? How did you respond?
2. What surprised you? What challenges arose? What successes did you have?
3. What questions or thoughts were you left thinking about?
4. Did you have any aha moments? Based on your experience, have you rethought any of the ideas below? If so, how?
    - Peer to peer relationships
    - Teacher-student relations
    - Parent-teacher relations
    - Classroom culture
    - School culture
    - Instruction
    - Other

# Section 8: Fostering Systems of Change

# Putting It All Together: Fostering Systems of Change

*There's no question that these tasks are easier if administrators are on board, even if they're not leading the charge. But my experience is that the impetus for change can come from many different people. (Greene, 2008, p. 231)*

**Fostering Systems of Change**

Ultimately, the cultivation of social-emotional competence in kids has implications that reach beyond the classroom. It has the potential to shape and shift school culture and climate. Individual teachers and individual kids meeting success translates into a reduction in challenging behaviors, increase in intrinsic motivation, and ultimately the setting of the stage for academic achievement.

While social-emotional competence equals happy and productive kids, it's also true that, with effort, social-emotional competence leads to a happy and productive school culture.

We've talked with teachers who have begun infusing social-emotional competence into current school structures and we've spoken with teachers who wish to expand its implementation. Below, you'll find a list of steps to take to begin the process of moving social-emotional competence beyond the classroom environment.

**Planning Phase:**

**Seek Out Support**: Identify individuals who can inspire change, who can identify the school's readiness for change, and who have the commitment and will to set goals and change minds through education. Begin talking with these folks about what you notice about both adult and child behavior and ways to shift both positively. These colleagues can include school psychologists, administrative assistants, janitor, afterschool personnel, parents, and even students.

**Analyze and Create Structures:** Often we get stuck in the same way of doing things without analyzing and/or reconsidering the efficacy and usefulness of practice. With your like-minded team, look at structures in the school that easily support the development of social-emotional competence (i.e. advisory, morning meetings, independent reading). Create a plan of action. In addition, look for ways to create new structures or practices that support the cultivation of social-emotional intelligence (i.e. classroom rules and procedures, cafeteria set-up etc.).

**Enlist the Help of Leadership:** There is no question that leadership makes a difference. Identify key administrator inside and outside of your building who are willing to collaborate and explore change. Invite them into conversations and/or events as colleagues and participants.

**Key Implementation Questions** *from Greene (2008, p. 233)*
1. Should implementation begin as a pilot program with individual students and/or teachers?
2. How will we train staff?
3. Should initial implementation occur in selected classrooms, grades, learning communities, or teams?
4. Should participation in training occur on a voluntary basis or as a school-wide initiative?
5. What are the best mechanisms for ongoing training and teamwork so as to ensure the sustainability of the effort?

**Implementation Phase:** Below are some ways in which current teachers, administrators, and caregivers have begun to change systems using the Mariposa Model.

1. Integrate social-emotional competence into discussions and 'care' plans, such as IEPs, BIPs for students.
2. During team meetings, use Cooperative Problem Solving to identify key issues that you are seeing school-wide, grade-wide, or team-wide. In this way everyone becomes acclimated to the process and is able to see the benefits of the process before using it with kids.
3. Incorporate key processes, such as identifying lagging skills, Empathy, Personal Message, and Cooperative Problem Solving in team discussions.
4. Begin a reading group or book club that studies SEC and creates 'action' plans to be used with individual students, whole student groups, or throughout the school. (i.e., to address transitions between classes, recess)
5. Create a 'care' package for the teachers who will teach some of your more challenging students the following year. Be open with your process and share with them what works in managing a particular student's challenging behaviors.
6. Invite Mariposa to give a talk, speak with the principal, or host a class.

**Reflection and Improved 'Practice' Phase:**

1. Make time to meet and authentically to discuss how things are going. What challenges have arisen? What success have you had? Did you discover new ways to support kids or integrate SEC into the classroom? Share your practices, emotions, and opinions.
2. Assess structures and teams. Have honest conversations about the needs of the schools, the needs of team members. Revisit goals often.

There are numerous ways to infuse social-emotional competence into school culture. Ideally, you would want to start at the beginning of the year and have total school buy-in. However, what is ideal isn't always practical, and change often begins with the few rather than the many. Regardless of how you start, with consistency, effort, and teamwork, you can create a dynamic of social-emotional competence in your community. That single dynamic has the potential to transform school climates and beyond.

# Appendix

# The Sequence of Skills

## Empathy

Definition: Communicating an understanding and acceptance of the feelings behind a child's words, actions, or point of view; the ability to understand and label a child's emotions or underlying needs/motivation

Mechanics of Empathy
1. Listen to the child's expressions
2. Identify the child's feelings/point of view
3. Phrase a statement that conveys acceptance and understanding of the child's feelings/point of view

Example:

**Child's Expression**: *"That dumb old teacher! She is always picking on me and I don't do anything."*

**Feelings/Point of View:** Unfairness, anger, hurt

**Empathic Response:** *"You think the teacher is being unfair and that really makes you mad."*

## Personal Message

Definition: Communication of one's own needs and feelings in a manner that is respectful and most likely to be heard or understood. Communicating your feelings and thoughts about a child's behavior in this manner helps children see things from your perspective.

Mechanics of Personal Message
1. Describe the child's behavior
2. State how you feel or how the behavior affects you

**If appropriate, you can identify what you want the child to do instead

Example:

**Child's Expression**: *"I hate doing homework. I don't understand why we need to learn this stuff."*

**Feelings/Point of View (of Yourself):** You want your child to enjoy learning; you are worried or frustrated that he or she is not learning.

**Personal Message:** *"When you do not finish your homework, I get worried that you will fall behind. I would like you to complete all the items on your worksheet."*

## Cooperative Problem Solving

Definition: Working with children to identify goals, dissect problems, and strategize for success.

Mechanics of Cooperative Problem Solving
1. **D**escribe the problem
2. **I**dentify goals and invite child to find a solution
3. Brain**S**torm **S**olutions
4. **E**valuate options
5. **C**hoose a plan
6. **T**ouch back

Example:

| | | |
|---|---|---|
| **D** | **D**escribe the problem: | "I notice that people interrupt and criticize each other during my lessons." |
| **I** | **I**dentify goals: | "I want to work together to stop these interruptions/put-downs." |
| **SS** | Brain**S**torm **S**olutions: | "Do you have any ideas?" |
| **E** | **E**valuate options: | "Your first two ideas are good, but the third one is the best for everyone." |
| **C** we | **C**hoose a plan: | "Instead of put-downs, we will use respectful talk from a list made." |
| **T** | **T**ouch back: | "Let's touch back next week and see if this plan is working for everyone." |

## Descriptive Reinforcement

Definition: Describing a child's actions and efforts and explaining their relevance to social-emotional skills to increase desired behaviors

Mechanics of Descriptive Reinforcement
1. Describe what the child did or did not do in *positive* behavior terms.
2. Identify the effort it took for the child to behave in this manner and how the behavior affected you.

**Remember that repetition and timeliness are important!

Example:
Child's statement: "I carried my books all the way home."
Ineffective adult response: "You are so strong!"

**Descriptive Reinforcement Response:** *"Those books were heavy—that took a lot of strength."*

## Inductive Discipline

Definition: Guiding a child's behavior by introducing appropriate limits and setting up logical consequences while explaining the rationales that support them

Mechanics of Inductive Discipline
1. Describe the child's behavior
2. State the rule or expectation *positively*
3. Give a warning: If the child breaks the rule, explain what will happen if the rule/limit is broken again
4. Implement a consequence: If the child breaks the rule/limit again, enforce the rule/limit by imposing the consequence you had previously warned the child about

Example: Your child continually interrupts you while you are on the phone.
**Positive Statement of Behavior:** "You are talking to me while I am on the phone."
**Rule:** "When I am on the phone, you must use a quiet voice and wait until I am finished to ask me any questions."

If the child continues to interrupt…
**Give a Warning**: "The next time you interrupt me while I am on the phone, I will go into another room and shut the door." (Note: Your choice of consequences may depend on the child's need. In this case, he or she will not be getting any attention if you are in another room with the door closed.)

If the child continues to interrupt…
**Implement a Consequence:** "You are too loud and I cannot hear. I am going into my room and closing the door."

# Recommended Reading

### Parent, Teacher, and Adult Resources

*Building Academic Success on Social and Emotional Learning: What Does the Research Say?*
By Zins, Weissberg, Wang, & Walberg (2004). Teachers College Press.

*The Developing Mind: How Relationships and the Brain Interact to Shape Who We Are*
By Daniel Siegel, M.D. (2001). The Guilford Press.

*Difficult Conversations: How to Discuss What Matters Most*
By Douglas Stone, Bruce Patton, & Sheila Heen (2000). Penguin.

*The Explosive Child*
By Dr. Ross Greene (1998), HarperCollins Publishers.

*How to Talk So Kids Can Learn at Home and in School*
By A. Faber & E. Mazlish (1995), Scribner.

*How to Talk So Kids Will Listen and Listen So Kids Will Talk*
By A. Faber & E. Mazlish (2004), Perennial Currents.

*Lost at School*
By Ross Greene, Ph.D. (2008). Scribner.

*Mindset, the New Psychology of Success*
By C.S. Dweck (2008), Random House Inc.

*Parenting: A Skills Training Manual*
By Dr. Louise Guerney (1995), Relationship Press.

*The Pressured Child: Freeing Our Kids from Performance Overdrive and Helping Them Find Success in School and Life*
By Michael Thompson (2005). Ballentine Books.

*Raising an Emotionally Intelligent Child*
By John Gottman, Ph.D. (1998). Simon & Schuster.

*Treating Explosive Kids:*
By Ross Greene, Ph.D. and J. Stuart Ablon (2005). The Guilford Press.

*Why Do They Act That Way?: A Survival Guide To The Adolescent Brain for You and Your Teen*
By David Walsh (2004). Free Press.

*Your Child's Self-Esteem: The Key to Life*
By D.C. Briggs (1975), Doubleday Press.

### Parent, Teacher, and Adult Resources for Bullying

*Best Friends, Worst Enemies: Understanding the Social Lives of Children*
By Michael Thompson & Catherine O'Neill Grace. (2001). Ballantine Books.

*Bullying in Schools and What to Do About It*
By Ken Rigby (1997). Jessica Kingsley Publishers.

*Bullying Prevention and Intervention: Realistic Strategies for Schools*
By S. Swearer, D.L. Espelage & S. Napolitano (2009), Guilford Press.

*The Bullying Prevention Handbook: A Guide for Principals, Teachers, and Counselors*
By John H. Hoover & Ronald L. Oliver (1996). National Education Service.

*The Bully Free Classroom: Over 100 Tips and Strategies for Teachers K–8*
By Allan L. Beane (1999). Free Spirit Publishing.

*Bullyproof Your Child For Life: Protecting Your Child From Teasing, Taunting, and Bullying for Good*
By Joel Haber & Jenna Glatzer (2007). Penguin Group, Inc.

*Childhood Bullying, Teasing, and Violence: What School Personnel, Other Professionals, and Parents Can Do*, 2nd Edition
By Dorothea M. Ross (2003). American Counseling Association.

*Games Children Play: How Games and Sport Help Children Develop*
By Kim Brooking-Payne (1997). Hawthorn Press.

*Letters to a Bullied Girl: Messages of Healing and Hope*
By Olivia Gardner (2008). Harper Publishers.

*Odd Girl Out*
By Rachel Simmons (2002). Harcourt Books.

*Peer Rejection: Developmental Processes and Intervention Strategies*
By Karen L. Bierman (2004). Guilford Press.

*Queen Bees and Wannabes: Helping Your Daughter Survive Cliques, Gossip, Boyfriends, and Other Realities of Adolescence*
By Rosalind Wiseman (2002). Three Rivers Press.

*Who's Afraid…?: Facing Children's Fears with Folktales*
By Norma J. Livo (1994). Libraries Unlimited, Inc.

## Stories for Young Children about Bullying and Teasing

*Arthur's April Fool*
By Marc Brown (1985). Little, Brown, & Company.

*Best Best Friends*
By Margaret Chodos-Irvine. Harcourt, Inc.

*Best Friends for Frances*
By Russell Hoban (1969). HarperCollins Children's Books.

*The Berenstain Bears and the Bully*
By Stan Berenstein & Jan Berenstein (1993). Random House.

*Bully*
By Judith Caseley (2001). Greenwillow Books.

*Chrysanthemum*
By Kevin Henkes (1991). Greenwillow Books.

*Enemy pie*
By Derek Munson (2000). Chronicle Books (2000).

*Fox in Love*
By Edward Marshall (1982). Puffin Books.

*George and Martha*
By James Marshall (1972). Houghton Mifflin Company.

*Just Kidding*
Written by Trudy Ludwig, Illustrated by Adam Gustavson (2006). Tricycle Press.

*Lucy and the Bully*
By Claire Alexander (2008). Gullane Children's Books.

*Say Something*
Written by Peggy Moss, Illustrated by Lea Lyon (2004). Tilbury House Publishers.

*Simon's Hook: A Story About Teases and Put-Downs*
Written by Karen Gedig Burnett, Illustrated by Laurie Barrows (1999). GR Publishing.

## Books for Older Children and Teens about Bullying and Teasing

*Bullies Are a Pain in the Brain*
By Trevor Romain (1997). Free Spirit Publishing.

*Cliques, Phonies, and Other Baloney*
By Trevor Romain (1998). Free Spirit Publishing.

*Crash*
By Jerry Spinelli (1996). Alfred A. Knopf, Inc.

*The Hundred Dresses*
Written by Eleanor Estes, Illustrated by Louis Slobodkin (1994). Harcourt, Inc.

*Letters to a Bullied Girl: Messages of Healing and Hope*
By Olivia Gardner (2008). Harper Publishers.

*Stick Up for Yourself: Every Kid's Guide to Personal Power and Positive Self-Esteem*
By Gershen Kaufman, Lev Raphael, & Pamela Espeland (1999). Free Spirit Publishing Inc.

*Odd Girl Out: The Hidden Culture of Aggression in Girls*
By Rachel Simmons (2002). Harcourt Books.

*Queen Bees and Wannabes: Helping Your Daughter Survive Cliques, Gossip, Boyfriends, and Other Realities of Adolescence*
By Rosalind Wiseman (2002). Three Rivers Press.

# Sample Answers
## 15 Challenging Characters

EMPATHY, PERSONAL MESSAGE, AND COOPERATIVE PROBLEM SOLVING ANSWERS

---

**Example**

Negative Nancy tends to expect the worst.

**Child Statement:** *"Why should I even bother raising my hand? You never call on me."*

**Empathic response:** *"You don't see the point of trying when you already know it is not going to work."*

**Personal Message:** *"I really value your input Nancy. I was not aware that I was not calling on you as much as the other students."*

Cooperative Problem Solving:
4. *"I notice that you are not raising your hand as much as usual. What's up?"*
5. *"I would like to help you learn ways to think more positively, even when you feel like there is no use in trying. Do you have any suggestions?*
6. *"Do you have any suggestions?"*
   a. Nancy could make a list of all the things that she is grateful for and turn these in at the end of the day.
   b. Nancy could keep a journal to become more aware of her thoughts.
   c. Nancy could make a list of behaviors she avoids as a result of expecting the worse and try at least 2 per day.
4. Nancy might not keep up with a journal. Nancy may make a list of things she will try, but may need the teacher to see this so that she can monitor her efforts. She may not have time during school to do this.
5. *"Moving forward, you will use the first five minutes of study hall each afternoon to write down your thoughts. If these are negative, rephrase them into positive expectations (hopes/wishes). If these are some behaviors that you have been avoiding, identify them and try at least one of them tomorrow. I will check your ideas briefly after study hall and then again at the end of the week so we can discuss how this is working."*

---

1. Shy Shonda has sat alone for lunch for the past couple weeks. Noticing her sad face, you ask how she is doing.

   **Child Statement and/or Behavior:** *"I'm fine. I don't like them anyhow – my real friends are at my other school."*

   **Empathic Response:** *"Part of you would rather sit alone than have to sit with students who are not your true friends."*… *"It is easier to be alone than to have to make new friends."*… *"You feel like they already have their friends and it's hard to be the new girl."*

   **Personal Message:** *"It's important to me that you feel welcome and included here. Even though it is not your old school, I hope that you will come to like it here."*

   **Cooperative Problem Solving:**

1. *"I have noticed that you have been sitting alone during lunch."*
2. *"I would like us to figure out a way to involve you in more interactions with the other students."*
3. *"Do you have any ideas?"*
    a. You could hold a show-and-tell in order for the students to get to know something more personal about each other. It would give Shonda a chance to show her personality to the rest of the class.
    b. During group projects, you could create the groups instead of the children choosing them. This way, no one, including Shonda, is left out.
    c. You could talk to Shonda and another child's parent about having a play date outside of school.
    d. Every day Shonda will talk to at least 5 different people and start making a list of what she says to them.
    e. Every time Shonda is sitting alone during class activity, she must go up to at least one student and start a conversation or ask if she can join them.
4. Shonda could be denied by another student, hurting her confidence even further. Shonda may get embarrassed that her mother is arranging play dates for her.
5. *"Moving forward I will be looking for more opportunities to pair you with some other students who I think you will get along well with. I will also be better at anticipating those times when you may end up working alone and pair you with a partner early on. Every day you will talk to at least 5 different people and start making a list of what you say to them and how you feel after talking with them."*

2. Hyperactive Harry is constantly getting out of his chair.

   **Child Statement**: *"I need to sharpen my pencil. Can I just sharpen it really quickly?"*

   **Empathic Response**: *"It is hard to continue working when your pencil is not sharpened. When something is bothering you, it is very hard to sit still."*

   **Personal Message**: *"It is hard for me to teach the class when you keep getting out of your chair."*

   **Cooperative Problem Solving:**
   1. *"I notice that it is very hard for you to sit still during class."*
   2. *"I would like to work together to figure out a way that you can remain in your chair through an entire lesson even though when you feel restless."*
   3. *"What do you think might help you remain in your seat?"*
       a. Harry could figure out a way to move in his chair in a way that is not disturbing to other children. (For example, you could put Velcro under his desk and rub it when he feels he needs to move.)
       b. Build in a mid-lesson stretch.
       c. Create a reward system for Harry. For example, for every 10 minutes he remains in his chair he gets a sticker.
       d. Build physical activity into the lesson.

4. A mid-lesson stretch may work for some children but could be distracting to others and interfere with problem solving. Keeping track of the minutes may be hard and inadvertently shift Harry's focus onto the minutes as opposed to the lesson.

5. *"Moving forward, when you are feeling restless and want to move, you will either squeeze your stress ball or rub the Velcro under your desk. I will try to incorporate movement into our lessons so that you will have a chance to move while still concentrating. I will also give you a chance to give some ideas on how to integrate movement into our lessons. Let's try this for this week and check back on Monday to see how it works."*

3. Picked-on Paul has repeatedly come back from recess complaining of being called names by the other children.

   **Child Statement and/or Behavior**: *"Jimmy keeps calling me a baby right in front of everyone!"*

   **Empathic Response**: *"You want him to stop but he just keeps picking on you!"*

   **Personal Message:** *"I am angry that he is treating you like that. I want to help figure out a way to put an end to this."*

   **Cooperative Problem Solving:**
   1. *"This has been going on for a while now. It seems like almost every day you come back from recess having been called names or picked on in other ways."*
   2. (Reiterate last part of Personal Message). *"I would like to work together to figure out a way to stop them from picking on you."*
   3. *"Do you have any ideas?"*
      a. Speak with Paul's parents about arranging play dates with other children.
      b. Be sure to find ways for Paul to sit and work closely with other children in the class.
      c. Speak with Paul's parents about arranging a play date with 1 of the children who are doing the name-calling.
      d. Recommend books to Paul and his parents on bullying as well as build these stories into story time in class. (For example, recommend that Paul's parents read "Enemy Pie" to Paul prior to the play date with one of the children engaging in the name calling.)
   4. The play date with the child conducting the teasing may heighten the conflict between the two children. Paul's parents may not view the bullying as a problem and/or they may view the problem as something that Paul is/is not doing to provoke the behavior.
   5. (The first step would be to ask the Paul how he feels about you working with his parents to set up some play dates with other students.) *"Moving forward, I will tell some stories in class that might act as a starting point to discussing the ways that we act towards each other in the classroom. I am also going to rearrange the seating in the class so that I can separate you from the children that are bullying, and separate them from each other."*

4. Even Steven thinks that you have it out for him. During math you notice him nudge another classmate. When you address him about his behavior, he gets very defensive.

**Child Statement**: *"He did it first! How come you always punish me and do nothing to him?"*

**Empathic Response:** *"You feel like I have it out for you."*

**Personal Message**: *"I don't want to make you feel like I have it out for you. I am just frustrated and not sure what to do to get you and others to stop disrupting the class."*

**Cooperative Problem Solving:**
1. *"I notice that when I catch you misbehaving, you feel that I am unfairly picking on you. What's up?"*
2. *"How can we figure out a way for you to manage your own behaviors without me becoming involved?"*
3. *"Do you have any ideas?"*
    a. Track (with a signal to Steven) the times when he is being disruptive. Count these and compare daily.
    b. If you do not call him out in public, he will refrain from defending his behavior out loud.
    c. Plan daily check in with Steven so that he has time to explain himself or things that provoke him.
    d. Move Steven to the front.
4. Steven may feel that moving to front is a punishment. Steven may also feel as though having to meet with him is further punishment and therefore not fair.
5. *"From now on when I notice that you are being disruptive, I will touch my pencil to my head and you will write a tally mark in your workbook. At the end of the day we will set aside some time to talk about how this is going and make any changes we need to continue supporting each other."*

5. Impulsive Isaac keeps getting in trouble for starting fights.

    **Child Statement and/or Behavior**: *"I won't hit anyone again, I promise."*

    **Empathic Response**: *"This time you mean it."*

    **Personal Message**: *"I am very frustrated that this keeps happening and am not sure what to do to help you."*

    **Cooperative Problem Solving:**
    1. *"Even though you really want to stop getting in fights, something happens in that moment when you are angry and the fight just happens."*
    2. *"How can we figure out a way such that you can control yourself even when you are mad and feel like fighting?"*
    3. *"Do you have any ideas?"*
        a. Tell Isaac to avoid those children that he fights with most often.
        b. Talk with his parents about ways to help cope with anger at home.
        c. Work with Isaac to identify and label feelings before they explode.
        d. Teach Isaac about "Fight or Flight" and help him identify situations with these types of reactions.
        e. Come up with a plan of alternative behaviors when he anticipates anger exploding.

4. Parents may not be sympathetic to Isaac's plight. They may also believe that punishment is the best solution. It may be hard to allocate time to teach and work with Isaac individually.

5. *"Moving forward, you will work with the guidance counselor for a half an hour, 2 mornings a week. She will give you some tools to help you learn better ways to get your needs met and point across (even when kids don't listen) without hitting. The three of us will check back at the end of the week to see how things are going."*

6. Frustrated Frederika has difficulty understanding math. During one of your lessons you notice that she is not participating. You walk over to her and inquire why she is not participating in the lesson.

    **Child Statement and/or Behavior**: (Staring out the window) *"I can't get any of these stupid math problems."*

    **Empathic Response:** *"You are so discouraged and feel like giving up."*

    **Personal Message**: *"I want to make this less frustrating for you – I am wondering what I can do to help."*

    **Cooperative Problem Solving:**
    1. *"I noticed that you stopped working on your math. What's up?"*
    2. *"How can we help you so that you can finish your assignment?"*
    3. *"Do you have any ideas?"*
        a. Break down the math problems into smaller, more understandable steps so that Fredericka can work through every problem herself.
        b. Pair her with another student who excels in math and will enjoy helping Fredericka.
        c. Twice a week, send Frederika to get extra help in math.
        d. Work with Frederika to identify an area of strength in another subject area or activity. Pair her with a student who is challenged in that area.
        e. Create games and activities within your lesson that target her weak spots in math.
    4. Frederika already has tutoring and dreads going. She might feel embarrassed about being singled out for extra help.
    5. *"We're going to try a different approach. Instead of giving you one long problem, I am going to break down each problem into sections. If you have worked on a problem for more than 20 minutes, then you should stop and move on to the next one. We will cover the difficult problem in extra help. Also, Billy will be your partner for pairs work. This is a chance to work on anything that you had trouble with earlier in the week."*

7. Lonely Laura is often left out.

    **Child Statement:** *"No one wants me in their group– it is because I look weird!"*

    **Empathic Response:** *"You think they don't want you in their group because of the way you look and that really hurts your feelings."*

**Personal Messages:** *"I do not think that that is why you are not in a group. I wish you could see all that beauty that I see in you."*

**Cooperative Problem Solving:**
1. *"I notice that you have been feeling really left out lately. You have been sitting by yourself a lot."*
2. *"What can we do so that you have more people to play with?"*
3. *"Do you have any ideas?"*
    a. During group projects, you could create the groups instead of the children choosing them. This way, no one, including Laura, is left out.
    b. Talk to Laura and another child's parent about having a play date outside of school.
    c. Every day Laura will talk to at least 5 different people and start making a list of what she says to them.
    d. Read a book in class or recommend a book to Laura about a child with a learning disability or physical difference who learns to accept themselves for who they are.
4. At this time, it is hard to foresee any obstacles.
5. *"There are several things that I think might help. From now on, we will have assigned partners so that all of the students can have a chance to work with different classmates. I would also recommend that you and Sally arrange a play date outside of school. Finally, here is a list of books about children very similar to you that have struggled with loneliness and have figured out ways to feel more included. Let's check back next week and see how everything goes."*

8. Comparing Carlos is continually sizing himself up against other classmates. After handing back the test from the previous day, you overhear him asking another student what he got on the exam.

    **Child Statement:** *"I got all of the problems right! What grade did you get Joel?"*

    **Empathic Response:** *"You want to know if Joel did as well as you did."*

    **Personal Message:** *"It is important to me that my students support one another. Telling Joel that you got them all right and then asking him what he got is not being supportive. Next time please refrain from comparing you grades with others."*

    **Cooperative Problem Solving:**
    1. *"You've been asking other students to share their grades with you even when I asked you not to. Why is it that you keep comparing yourself to the other students?"*
    2. *"Do you have any ideas on how you can keep your grade to yourself even though you really want to know what other students got? "*
    3. *"Do you have any ideas?"*
        a. Score and give feedback via the Internet.
        b. As a start, explore in more depth reasons why Carlos only feels accomplished when he is performing better than others (External locus of control). Then help him identify ways to increase internal locus of control.
        c. List with Carlos other ways to be acknowledged/valued that do not involve hurting others inadvertently.

d. Put Carlos in a role where he is helping other students prepare for their own test.

4. Other students may not want his help. By digging deeper and bringing up the reason why he is competitive might make him more vulnerable to criticism. By bringing this to his attention, you may have inadvertently increased his need to compare himself.

5. *"So the plan is that we will be returning tests via the Internet. Those who scored well on certain answers will be identified ahead on time and will be responsible for explaining their answers to the class the next day. Carlos, could you please keep a record of those times when you feel that one-upper worm creeping in and write down what you hope to accomplish by letting that worm out. Let's check back next week to see how this is going."*

9. Uncertain Ursula has a hard time working independently. She frequently asks for feedback when working on a project even though you have communicated the importance of trying first, then asking if you get stuck.

   **Child Statement:** *"Mr. Jones, I need some help. Is this right? Am I doing this the way I am supposed to?"*

   **Empathic Response:** *"You want some reassurance that you are on the right track."*

   **Personal Message:** *"I get annoyed when you ask for help when I asked you to give the problem a try before asking for my help."*

   **Cooperative Problem Solving:**
   1. *"I notice that you do not like to continue working on a task unless you have been told that you are doing it correctly. Why is that Ursula?"*
   2. *"I would like to figure out a way for you to complete a whole project without asking for my help- even when you may be wrong."*
   3. *"Do you have any ideas?"*
      a. Have Ursula write down her questions in the margin, give it her best shot, and then move on to the next question.
      b. Reassure Ursula that she will not be penalized if gets the answer wrong as long as she goes back and corrects her mistakes.
      c. Pair Ursula with another student who is patient and will answer her questions if necessary.
   4. Pairing Ursula with another student may not help her overcome her need for reassurance. This may also place unnecessary stress on the other student.
   5. *"Tomorrow we will start our new plan. During our independent projects you will write down all of your questions in the margin when you are unsure if you are on the right track. Having written the questions down you will continue working on the problem until you have completed the entire assignment. Before handing in your work, I will come by your desk and answer your questions. You will also have a chance to correct your work and turn your answers back in without being penalized."*

10. Anxious Amanda loves soccer but is concerned about this week's tryouts.

    **Child Statement:** *"I don't want to try out. My stomach hurts."*

    **Empathic Response:** *"You are nervous about tryouts and do not want to go."*

**Personal Message:** *"I don't want you to miss out on an activity you might really enjoy because you are nervous. On the other hand, I do not want to force you to play if you really don't want to."*

**Cooperative Problem Solving:**
1. *"You are so worried about trying out that it is making you feel physically sick and you don't even want to play."* (Note: Empathy can be used to describe the problem.)
2. *"How can we figure out a way for you to participate in activities in spite of your feeling so anxious?"*
3. *"Do you have any ideas?"*
   a. Verbally describe the concern and rate it on a 10 point scale.
   b. Have her list all the reasons why she might do well.
   c. Come up with a list of things/activities she will do if she does not make the team.
   d. List the things that she has control over vs. things she does not have control over.
4. Listing other activities may increase her anxiety because no other activity appeals to her as much as soccer.
5. *"From now on, when you are feeling anxious, you will first rate the severity of your feeling on a scale from 1 to 10. Next, identify on paper or verbally all the reasons why you are likely to succeed at the task. Then we will check back and see if this helps bring your anxiety down."*

11. You learn that a fight broke out in school. One child got beaten up while the others watched and did nothing. Bystander Billy saw what took place but is refusing to tell the name of the bully.

    **Child Statement and/or Behavior:** *"What am I supposed to do, be a snitch?"*

    **Empathic Response:** *"You are torn, while you know we need you to tell us the name of the child, you're worried that if you do tell you could end up in the same boat as the victim."*

    **Personal Message:** *"I am so upset that this happened and want make certain that it doesn't happen again. I wish that children who stood watching would have felt empowered to take action."*

    **Cooperative Problem Solving:**
    1. *"You witnessed another child being bullied but did not want to report this out of fear that you could become the bully's next victim or become ostracized at school."* (Note the use of Empathy to describe the problem.)
    2. *"I want to figure out a way to be both speak out and stay protected at the same time."* (Note that this is a rewording of the Personal Message.)
    3. *"Do you have any ideas?"*
       a. Set up an anonymous reporting system.
       b. Announce that you are accepting email accounts of the incident.
       c. Take away class privileges until the offender confesses or witnesses come forward.
       d. Develop a reward system to increase group incentives for reporting bullying and pro-social behavior.

    e. Involve the whole class in brainstorming ideas about reducing bullying.

4. Taking away privileges may cause retaliation against the victim. Similarly, rewards to the witness may bring unwanted attention to that student.

5. *"From now on we are going to implement several bullying reduction strategies including: 1) An anonymous reporting system will be established; 2) a weekly report of local current events that display acts of kindness and courage; 3) diversity education in the classroom to celebrate differences and promote tolerance."*

12. Forgetful Felix has a hard time remembering to bring his homework folder back to school.

    **Child Statement**: *"Please don't be mad at me – I forgot my binder again!"*

    **Empathic Response:** *"You are trying to remember your folder but you just keep forgetting! It is very discouraging for you and you are worried you are in trouble."*

    **Personal Message:** *"It is frustrating for me that you forget your homework because I want you to be able to participate in class."*

    **Cooperative Problem Solving:**
    1. *"You keep forgetting your homework despite your efforts to remember."*
    2. *"I want to figure out a system that will make it easy for you to bring your homework."*
    3. *"Do you have any ideas?"*
    Communicate with Felix's parents to do the following:
    a. Put the binder in the car after homework is finished.
    b. Make up a rhyme to recite in the morning to remember all school belongings.
    c. Fasten homework binder to something (like lunch) that makes it to school every day.
    d. Put a sign on the front door at home.
    4. Felix leaves the binder in the car. Child does not ride in the car, he takes the bus. There is not anything that goes to school on a regular basis.
    5. *"Starting this afternoon, when you are finished your homework you will put your binder in your backpack and put the backpack in to the car (or by the front door). Let's check back at the end of this week and see how this works for you."*

13. Today after school is the school play and everyone is excited about it. Chatty Charlie and Talkative Tom are talking about this in the back of your class. You interrupt class and nicely ask them to stop.

    **Child Statement and/or Behavior**: Both students acknowledge your comment with a nod. However, when you begin teaching they continue their conversation.

    **Empathic Response:** *"It is hard to stay quiet because you are so excited about the school play."*

    **Personal Message:** *"It is very hard for me to finish the lesson when there is so much talking. It is very frustrating for me because I've already asked you to be quiet many times."*

    **Cooperative Problem Solving:**

1. *"You have not been able to refrain from talking to each other during class."*
2. *"What can we do to help you remain quiet without having to have me stop class to ask you to stop talking?"*
3. *"Do you have any ideas?"*
    a. Separate Charlie and Tom.
    b. Whole class has a point system where class begins with 10 points and they lose for talking. Reward is given at the end week if class stays within a certain point range.
    c. Teacher keeps after class if they are talking.
    d. Assign students extra homework is they are caught talking during the lesson.
4. Students have too much homework already. Teacher cannot keep students after class because of school policy.
5. *"Moving forward, we will separate you and Tom on the days of the school play. We will also adopt a class reward system to give everyone an incentive to remain quite during the lesson."*

14. Rigid Ralph is not happy about changes in seating.

    **Child Statement**: *"What happened to my desk? Why can't I just sit where I was before?"*

    **Empathic Response:** *"You are concerned and confused because you do not know why you have to change your seat. You would prefer that I left you where you were"*

    **Personal Message:** *"I would like to give every student a chance to work from all different seats in the room and with different students. I will work to help you adjust to your new arrangement."*

    **Cooperative Problem Solving:**
    1. *"You would prefer to stay in the same seat throughout the year even when I make seating changes periodically to the room."*
    2. *"I would like to figure out away to help you adjust to all of the seating changes throughout the year."*
    3. *"Do you have any suggestions for how to make this less stressful for you?"*
        a. Let Ralph sit next to the same students.
        b. Give Ralph several seating options to choose from.
        c. Give Ralph a heads up prior to changing the desk so that he can prepare himself.
        d. Allow Ralph to help you move the desks.
    4. All students will want to choose who they sit next to. Ralph might choose the same seat every time.
    5. *"Moving forward, I will let you know the day before making any seating changes and will let you help me rearrange the desks. You will be given 3 options for where to sit."*

15. Distractible Dante has a hard time completing any assignments because other things going on in the classroom distract him. You constantly are trying to encourage him to stay on track.

**Child Statement and/or Behavior:** During your math lesson, you notice Dante staring out the window and playing with his pencil.

**Empathic response:** *"It is hard to concentrate on school work when there are other things going on in the classroom and outside."*

**Personal Message:** *"I want to help you to finish an assignment without stopping or being distracted."*

## Cooperative Problem Solving:
1. *"It is very hard for you to pay attention through an entire lesson."* (Note use of Empathy to describe the problem).
2. *"I want to work together to figure out how to help you finish an assignment without stopping or being distracted."* (Note the use of a Personal Message to describe the goal.)
3. *"Do you have any ideas?"*
    a. Move Dante to the front of the room.
    b. Incorporate more physical activity into the lesson.
    c. Ask Dante for input in creating the exercises.
    d. Involve Dante in class discussion.
    e. Reward Dante when he completes a lesson independently.
4. Dante gets anxious when called on in class.
5. *"In order to help improve your ability to concentrate, we will move you to the front of the class. I will also try to include your ideas for making the exercises more interesting."*

## Descriptive Reinforcement Answers

1. Shonda has been more assertive lately. Today she approached some students and asked them if she could join them for lunch.

    **Descriptive Reinforcement:**
    *"While you were not sure if they would accept you, you took a chance and asked them anyhow."*

2. Harry has stayed in his chair through the entire lesson.

    **Descriptive Reinforcement:**
    *"Even though you wanted to get up, you stayed in your chair through the whole lesson without even asking if you could get up."*

3. Paul has managed to find other children to play with during recess. And, as a result, was not picked on by the usual kids.

    **Descriptive Reinforcement:**
    *"You tried something different and it worked! Those children treat you like you deserve to be treated."*

4. Following the assignment of the line leader of the week you notice that Steven is unfazed.

    **Descriptive Reinforcement:**
    *"You remembered that you do get your turn to be the leader too."*

5. Isaac has managed to keep his hands to himself during dodge ball, in spite of the fact that the opposing team cheated to win the game.

    **Descriptive Reinforcement:**
    *"Although you really wanted to hand it to them, you exerted self-control and managed to avoid getting into a fight!"*

6. During math, Fredericka has come to you for help instead of giving up on her math assignment.

    **Descriptive Reinforcement:**
    *"Although you were frustrated, you remained calm, followed our plan and came to me for help before giving up."*

7. Laura has been more focused on her art talents by putting her energy into her art project as opposed to thinking and talking about the way that she looks.

    **Descriptive Reinforcement:**
    *"You have been putting so much energy into your art – using your energy in a creative way seems to bring you a lot of joy."*

8. After handing back this weeks quiz, Carlos refrains from asking the other students how they did.

    **Descriptive Reinforcement:**

*"You refrained from telling the other children how you did. Your consideration of their feelings was stronger than your need to tell them how you did."*

9. Ursula has waited until her assignment was finished before asking you for feedback.

    **Descriptive Reinforcement:**
    *"Even though you were not sure you were on the right track, you persisted anyhow like we discussed. Thank you – that helps me to be able to help the other children. "*

10. Amanda decided to give soccer a try.

    **Descriptive Reinforcement:** *"Even though you were worried sick, you decided to give it a go and try out anyhow."*

11. Billy finally stood up to the bullying student.

    **Descriptive Reinforcement:** *"It takes a lot of courage to stand up to someone who scares you. Your compassion was stronger than your fear."*

12. Felix remembered to bring his homework folder back to school today.

    **Descriptive Reinforcement:** *"You remembered your homework binder!"*

13. Charlie and Tom refrained from talking during your English class.

    **Descriptive Reinforcement:** *"Even though you wanted to talk you each other, you both waited until I was finished. Thank you – I was able to finish the whole lesson!"*

14. Ralph decided to try working with a new lab partner without being asked.

    **Descriptive Reinforcement:** *"You went outside of your comfort zone and tried something different."*

15. Dante has finished his homework on time.

    **Child Statement**: *"Look, I'm all done!"*

    **Descriptive Reinforcement:** *"You concentrated on your work and did not stop until you were finished!"*

## INDUCTIVE DISCIPLINE ANSWERS

1) Shonda refuses to welcome the new student.

**Child Statement**: *"I don't care about the new student. Why should I go over there and say hi?"*

**Negative Communication:** *"It is not very nice to ignore the new student."*

   a) *"Please tell our visitor your name and shake her hand."*

   b) N

2) Harry gets up from his desk and proceeds to knock over the classroom display.

**Negative Communication**: *"How many times do I have to tell you to sit in your chair?"*

   a) *"Go back to your desk and sit down until the lesson is over."*

   b) Y (Natural)

   c) Pick up the knocked-over display.

3) Paul runs up to you after lunch and says that all the children were picking on him again.

**Negative Communication:** *"You shouldn't be a tattle-tale, Paul."*

   a) *"When the other children are picking on you, use your words kindly to ask them to stop. Try to resolve the issue on your own before coming to me."*

   b) N

4) Steven takes another student's pencil without asking. When you reprimand him, he gets defensive.

**Child Statement:** *"I don't have a pencil! How come you always punish me for no reason?"*

**Negative Communication:** *"Do not talk back to the teacher."*

   a) *"I need you to understand that I am reprimanding you for a reason. You need to follow the rules just as everyone else does."*

   b) Y

   c) Steven must give the pencil back to the student and apologize for touching his things.

5) Isaac throws another child on the ground claiming they took his ball without asking.

**Child Statement:** *"That thief stole my ball!"*

**Negative Communication:** *"Just because he took your ball does not mean that you can hit him!"*

   a) *"When someone takes something without asking, come and ask for help from an adult before acting out physically."*

   b) Y

   c) Loss of privilege to use the ball of a limited period of time.

6) Frederika copies another student's answers during a math quiz.

**Negative Communication:** *"Cheating is taken very seriously here."*

   a) *"Please turn in your own work even if it means that you may be wrong."*

   b) Y

   c) Frederika must retake a different quiz.

7) Laura lashes out by crying and stomping her feet because she was left out of group activities yet again.

**Child Statement**: *"I hate it here! I just want to go home!"*

**Negative Communication:** *"We do not throw a temper tantrum when things don't go our way."*

   a) *"Please use your words when you are feeling frustrated or upset so that we can work together to find a solution."*

   b) N

8) You overhear Carlos making fun of another student's athletic ability.

**Child Statement**: *"I don't think he could kick that ball over 3 feet!"*

**Negative Communication:** *"Do not make fun of other children."*

   a) *"Treat other students how you yourself would like to be treated."*

   b) Y

   c) Carlos apologizes to the student for making fun of him.

9) During an important test, Ursula raises her hand to ask for help. After you help her with one problem, she raises her hand again for help on the next problem.

**Negative Communication:** *"Do not ask me for help before you try the problem on your own. I will not always be here to help you."*

   a) *"It would be more beneficial to you to try to problem before asking for help because you need to learn the material on your own."*

   b) Y

   c) Before helping Ursula, she must prove to you that she tried the problem on her own.

10) Amanda fakes having a headache and asks to go to the nurse in order to avoid gym class.

**Negative Communication:** *"It is not right to pretend that you are sick when you really are fine."*

   a) *"Please tell the truth about when you are really sick. If you are feeling nervous about gym class come talk to me first before asking to go to the nurse."*

   b) N

11) Billy harasses another student out of fear of being ostracized.

**Child Statement:** *"Look at his big ears! He looks like Dumbo!"*

**Negative Communication:** *"Do not make fun of other children."*

   a) *"Please treat others like you want to be treated."*
   b) Y
   c) Billy must apologize to the student for calling him names. Also, Billy must sit out of play for 10 minutes.

12) Felix forgets to do his daily classroom chore, erasing the chalkboard, once again.

**Negative Communication:** *"If you don't start remembering to erase the chalkboard, I will give the chore to someone else."*

   a) *"Having a classroom chore is a big responsibility. If you try a little harder, I know that you can remember to do yours ever day."*
   b) Y
   c) Give Felix a warning. If he continues to forget, give the chore for someone else for the week.

13) Charlie talked to Tom throughout the guest speaker's lecture.

**Negative Communication:** *"We don't speak when others are speaking."*

   a) *"It is important to listen when others are speaking, especially when we have a guest in the classroom."*
   b) Y
   c) Separate Charlie and Tom so that they do not talk to each other.

14) Ralph throws a tantrum when he has to work with a new partner in science class.

**Child Statement:** *"This is so stupid! I like my old partner better!"*

**Negative Communication:** *"Ralph, when I assign something, you do what I say."*

   a) *"Please use your words when you are upset. It is important to work with new people and experience new things."*
   b) N

15) After assigning a handout 45 minutes ago, you realize that Dante has not even looked at it yet. He is too busy staring out the window at the cars passing by.

**Negative Communication**: *"Dante, why didn't you start your handout yet? You are wasting time!"*

   a) *"Please try to focus on getting your work done. It is important that you learn this material."*
   b) Y
   c) Move Dante's seat away from the window. Also, you could sit with him and go through the worksheet until he is finished.

# RESTATING THE RULES ANSWERS

|  | RULE/LIMIT | RE-STATE RULE/LIMIT POSITIVELY |
|---|---|---|
| Example | No running in the hallways. | Students must walk in the hallways. |
| 1 | No hitting. | Keep your hands to yourself. |
| 2 | No interrupting. | Raise your hand when you wish to speak. |
| 3 | No cheating. | Keep your eyes on your own paper and turn in your own work. |
| 4 | Do not steal other people's property. | Only take or use what is yours unless you ask first. |
| 5 | Do not damage other's property. | Treat other's property with respect and care. |
| 6 | Do not exclude or ignore others. | Include other classmates when you play. |
| 7 | Do not name call. | Speak kindly of others or not at all. |
| 8 | No lying. | Tell the truth. |
| 9 | Do not disturb other students when they are working. | Remain quiet until all other students have finished working. |
| 10 | Do not disturb the teacher when they are helping another student or teaching a lesson. | Raise your hand if you need help from the teacher. Refrain from getting out of your chair unless you have permission. |

**Additional Examples**

|  | | |
|---|---|---|
|  | Do not talk behind other people's backs. | If you have a concern with another student, address them directly or get help from an adult. |

# References

Adelman, H.S., & Taylor, L. (2005). Classroom climate. In S.W. Lee (Ed.), *Encyclopedia of school psychology.* Thousand Oaks, CA: Sage.

Alexander, K.L., Entwisle, D.R., Thompson, M.S. (1987). School performance, status relations, and the structure of sentiment: Bringing the teacher back in. *American Sociological Review; 52:*665–682.

Anderman, L.H., Anderman, E.M. (1999). Social predictors of changes in students' achievement goal orientations. *Contemporary Educational Psychology; 24*(10):21–37.

Beach, M.C., Moore, R.D., Roter, D.L., & Berkenblit, G.V. (2008, November). Building relationships in HIV care: The role of emotional dialogue. *The Johns Hopkins University Gazette, 38*(18).

Birch, S.H., & Ladd, G.W. (1997). The teacher-child relationship and children's early school adjustment. *Journal of School Psychology, 35*(1): 61–79.

Blum, R.W., & Libbey, H.P. (2004). School connectedness—Strengthening health and education outcomes for teenagers. *Journal of School Health, 74,* 229–299.

Bronson, M. (2000). Self-regulation in early childhood: Nature and nurture. New York: Guilford Press.

Bryk, A.S., & Schneider, B. (2002). *Trust in schools: A core resource for improvement.* New York: Russell Sage Foundation.

Catalano, R.F., Haggerty, K.P., Oesterle, S., Fleming, C.B., & Hawkins, J.D. (2004). The importance of bonding to school for healthy development: Findings from the Social Development Research Group. *Journal of School Health, 74,* 252-261.

Collaborative for Academic, Social and Emotional Learning (CASEL). (2010). *The benefits of school-based social and emotional learning programs.* [PDF document]. Retrieved from www.casel.org/search_results.php?cx=002793615769078246548%3A17kypcqsxpc&cof=FORID%3A11&q=The+Benefits+of+School-Based+Social+and+Emotional+Learning&sa=Search#1086

Collaborative for Academic, Social and Emotional Learning (CASEL). (2009a). *SEL: What is it and how does it contribute to students' academic success?* [Powerpoint slides]. Retrieved from www.casel.org/pub/dvds.php#powerpoint, Slide 4.

Collaborative for Academic, Social and Emotional Learning (CASEL). (2009b). *Social emotional learning and bullying prevention.* [PDF document]. Retrieved from www.casel.org/search_results.php?cx=002793615769078246548%3A17kypcqsxpc&cof=FORID%3A11&q=Social+Emotional+Learning+and+Bullying+Prevention&sa=Search#1037

Cooper, D.H., & Farran, D.C. (1991). *The Cooper-Farran behavioral rating scales.* Clinical Psychology Pub Co.

Davidson, R. (December 10, 2007). The heart-brain connection: The neuroscience of social, emotional, and academic learning. [Video Recording of Presentation]. Presentation at the CASEL Forum, New York, NY. Retrieved from: http://www.edutopia.org/richard davidson-sel-brain-video

*Dropout rate down nearly 60 percent since 2007; graduation rate up 10 percent* (2010, october 06). *Baltimore City Mayor's Office.* Retrieved from BaltCity.gov on January 3 2012.

Durlak, J.A., Weissberg, R.P., Dymnicki, A.B., Taylor, R.D., & Schellinger, K.B. (2008). Enhancing students' social and emotional learning promotes success in school: A meta-analysis. Manuscript submitted for publication.

Durlak, J.A., Weissberg, R.P., Dymnicki, A.B., Taylor, R.D., & Schellinger, K.B. (2011). The impact of enhancing students' social and emotional learning: A meta-analysis of school-based universal interventions. *Child Development, 82,* 474-501.

Entwisle D.R., & Alexander K.L. (1988). Factors affecting achievement test scores and marks of Black and White first graders. *Elementary School Journal; 88*:449–471.

Epstein, M., Atkins, M., Cullinan, D., Kutash, K., & Weaver, R. U.S. Department of Education, Institute of Educational Services. (2008). *Reducing behavior problems reducing behavior problems in the elementary school classroom in the elementary school classroom* (NCEE 2008-012) National Center for Education Evaluation and Regional Assistance.

Faber, A., & Mazlish, E. (2003). *How to talk so kids can learn: At home and in school*. New York, NY: Scribner.

Faber, A., & Mazlish, E. (1980). *How to talk so kids will listen & listen so kids will talk*. New York, NY: HarperCollins Publishing, Inc.

The Future of Children. School readiness: Closing racial and ethnic gaps. Princeton, NJ: The Woodrow Wilson School of Public and International Affairs at Princeton University and the Brookings Institution; (2005). Retrieved from http://www.futureofchildren.org/information2826/information_show.htm?doc_id=25598

Gottfredson, D.C., Gottfredson, G.D., & Hybl, L.G. (1993). Managing adolescent behavior: A multi-year, multi-school study. *American Educational Research Journal, 30,* 179-215.

Gottman, J. (1997). *Raising an emotionally intelligent child.* New York: Simon & Schuster Paperbacks.

Greene, R.W. (2011). *The explosive child: A new approach for understanding and parenting easily frustrated, chronically inflexible children*. New York: Harper Paperbacks.

Greene, R.W. (2009). *Lost at school: Why our kids with behavioral challenges are falling through the cracks and how we can help them*. (1st ed.) New York: Scribner Book Company.

Greene, R., & Ablon, J. (2006). *Treating explosive kids: The collaborative problem-solving approach*. New York: Guilford Press.

Hamre, B.K., & Pianta, R.C. (2001). Early teacher-child relationships and the trajectory of children's school outcomes through eighth grade. *Child Development* 72 (2): 625–638.

Hawkins, J.D., Catalano, R.F., Kosterman, R., Abbott, R., & Hill, K.G. (1999). Preventing adolescent health-risk behaviors by strengthening protection during childhood. *Arch Pediatr Adolesc Med 153*:226-234.

Hill, N.E., Castellino, D.R., Lansford, J.E., Nowlin, P., Dodge, K.A., Bates, J.E., Pettit, G.S. (2004). Parent academic involvement as related to school behavior, achievement, and aspirations: Demographic variations across adolescence. *Child Development;75*:1491–1509.

Hughes, J., & Kwok, O. (2007). Influence of student-teacher and parent-teacher relationships on lower achieving readers' engagement and achievement in the primary grades. *Journal of Educational Psychology, 99,* 39-51.

Jones, S.M., Brown, J.L., & Aber, J.L. (2008), *Changing schools and community organizations to foster positive youth development.* London: Oxford University Press.

Klem, M., & Connell, J.P. (2004, September). Relationships matter: Linking teacher support to student engagement and achievement. *Journal of School Health*, 74, 262-273. Retrieved from http://www.irre.org/publications/pdfs/Klem_and_Connell_2004_JOSH_article.pdf

Kohl, G.O.; Weissberg, R.P.; Reynolds, A.J.; Kasprow, W.J. (1994). Teacher perceptions of parent involvement in urban elementary schools: Sociodemographic and school adjustment correlates; Paper presented at the annual meeting of the American Psychological Association; Los Angeles, CA. 1994 Aug.

Ladd, G.W., Birch, S.H., & Buhs, E.S. (1999). Children's social and scholastic lives in kindergarten: Related spheres of influence? *Child Development,* 70 (6): 1373–1400.

McClelland, M.M., & Morrison, F.J. (2003). The emergence of learning-related social skills in preschool children. *Early Childhood Research Quarterly, 18* (2), 206-224.

Murdock, T., & Miller, A. (2003). Teachers as sources of middle school students' motivational identity: Variable-centered and person-centered analytic approaches. *The Elementary School Journal, 103*(4), 383-399.

Murray, C.B. (1996). Estimating achievement performance: A confirmation bias. *Journal of Black Psychology, 1996;* 22:67–85.

Murray, C., & Greenberg, M.T. (2000). Children's relationship with teachers and bonds with school: An Investigation of patterns and correlates in middle childhood. *Journal of School Psychology,* 38 (5): 423–445.

National Center for Education Statistics (2005). National assessment of educational progress: The nation's report card. U.S. Department of Education. Retrieved from http://nces.ed.gov/nationsreportcard/

NICHD Early Child Care Research Network. (2004). Trajectories of physical aggression from toddlerhood to middle childhood. *Monographs of the Society for Research in Child Development, 69,* vii–120.

Olweus, D. (1978). *Aggression in the schools: Bullies and whipping boys.* Washington, DC: Hemisphere.

Partenio, I., Taylor, R.L. (1985). The relationship of teacher ratings and IQ: A question of bias? *School Psychology Review, 1985;* 14:79–83.

Pianta, R.C., Steinberg, M.S., & Rollins, K.B. (1995). The first two years of school: Teacher-child relationships and deflections in children's classroom adjustment. *Development and Psychopathology,* 7 (2): 297–312.

Pianta, R.C.; Walsh, D.J. (1996). High-risk children in schools: Constructing sustaining relationships. New York: Routledge.

Pianta, R.C. (1997). Adult-child relationship processes and early schooling. *Early Education and Development,* 8(1): 11–26.

Pianta, R.C.; Rimm-Kauffman, S.E.; Cox, M.J. (1999). The transition to kindergarten. Baltimore, MD: Brookes Publishing.

Pianta, R.C., Hamre, B.K., & Stuhlman, M.W. (2003). Relationships between teachers and children. In *Educational Psychology*, Vol. 7 of *Comprehensive Handbook of Psychology*, ed. William M. Reynolds and Gloria E. Miller, 199–234. New York: Wiley.

Pollack, W. (1998) Real boys: Rescuing our sons from the myths of boyhood. New York: Henry Holt & Company, LLC.

Quest International. (1995). *Report for U.S Department of Education expert panel on safe, disciplined, and drug-free schools: Lions-Quest Skills for Growing*. Newark, OH: Author.

Raver, C.C., Jones, S., Li-Grining, C., Metzger, M., Smallwood, K., & Sardin, L. (2008). Improving preschool classroom processes: Preliminary findings, *Early Childhood Research Quarterly, 23,* 10-26.

Raver, C.C., Jones, S.M., Li-Grining, C.P., Zhai, F., Bub, K., & Pressler, E. (2011), CSRP's impact on low-income preschoolers' pre-academic skills: Self-regulation and teacher-student relationships as two mediating mechanisms. *Child Development, 82* (1)*,* 362-378.

Resnick, M.D., et al. (1997). Protecting adolescents from harm: Findings from the national longitudinal study of adolescent health. *Journal of the American Medical Association, 278* (10): 823–832.

Shonkoff, J.P., & Phillips, D. (Eds). (2000). From neurons to neighborhoods: The science of early childhood development. Washington, DC: National Academy Press.

Skinner, E., Belmont, M., (1993). Motivation in the classroom: Reciprocal effects of teacher behavior and student engagement across the school year. *Journal of Educational Psychology; 85:*571–581*.*

Teacher-Child Relationships. (2011). International Encyclopedia of the Social Sciences. 2008. *Encyclopedia.com.* (December 10, 2011). http://www.encyclopedia.com/doc/1G2-3045302709.html

Tobler, N., & Stratton, H. (1997) Effectiveness of school based drug prevention programs: A meta-analysis of the research. Journal of Primary Prevention, *18,* 71–128.

Townsend, A. (2006). *The impact of parenting practices and early childhood curricula on children's academic achievement and social competence.* Unpublished doctoral dissertation, University of Maryland, College Park, MD. (UMI Dissertation Services No. 3212679).

U.S. Department of Education, Office for Civil Rights, OCR Elementary and Secondary School Survey, 2002.

Wigfield, A., Eccles, J.S. (2000). Expectancy–value theory of achievement motivation. *Contemporary Educational Psychology, 25:*68–81. [PubMed: 10620382]

Zins, J.E., Weissberg, R.P., Wang, M.C., & Walberg, H.J. (Eds.). (2004). *Building academic success on social and emotional learning: What does the research say?* New York: Teachers College Press.

Zsolnai, L. (2002), Transatlantic business ethics. Business Ethics: A European Review, 11: 97–105. doi: 10.1111/1467-8608.00262